The Day-Tripper's Guide to New York City

to New York City

Visiting the City from the Suburbs

The Day-Tripper's Guide to New York City
Visiting the City from the Suburbs

Willa Speiser

Aylesworth
Press
Morristown,
New Jersey

The Day-Tripper's Guide to New York City
Visiting the City from the Suburbs

by Willa Speiser

Aylesworth Press
Morristown, New Jersey
Copyright © 2003 by Aylesworth Press

Aylesworth Press is an imprint of New Jersey Monthly Press

Manufactured in Canada

Library of Congress Catalog Control Number: 2002 11239

ISBN 1-893787-03-6

Cover design by George Foster, Foster & Foster Inc.

Interior design by Liz Tufte, Folio Bookworks

Photographs by Walter Choroszewski

The Day-Tripper's Guide to New York City

Visiting the City from the Suburbs

Contents

Introduction

Wherever you live and work, New York is an amazing resource, and all its suburban neighbors have to do is come over a bridge, through a tunnel, or simply cross the border from Nassau County into Queens. This book is meant to invite you to be a tourist for a day, with the luxury of going home at night and coming back the next day, next week, or whenever you choose.

Thousands of people from New Jersey, Connecticut, New York State, and even Pennsylvania who commute to New York City are tied to the metropolis by their jobs but don't necessarily spend much free time there. It's easy to forget that the PATH train or Metro-North car you ride every day is taking you to a legendary place that people thousands of miles away dream of visiting. And it's even harder to recall, after months or even years go by and you haven't been to the city, how easy it is to get there and how exciting it is once you arrive.

When I first discussed the idea for this book with Nancy Nusser, then editor of *New Jersey Monthly* magazine, and Kate Tomlinson, the magazine's publisher, it was the summer of 2001, and the city was filled with tourists, shops were bustling, new museums were thriving, theater was lively, and there was an over-all sense that New York City was a wonderful place to visit and maybe even to live, if you could afford it. After the terrorist attack on the World Trade Center on September 11, 2001, reality changed, as did the prevailing mood. New York City will never be quite the same as it was during the sunny summer of 2001; both its skyline and its sense of place and self have been changed. Some landmarks have been lost, but the city is still there, from the endlessly varied streetscapes that define each neighborhood to the botanical gardens of Brooklyn and the Bronx and the museums of Manhattan. New York is one of the great cities of the world, and those of us who are its neighbors are lucky to be able to explore it.

This book is organized geographically for the most part, except for several chapters that concentrate on special interests such as museums. That doesn't mean, however, that a day trip to the city from the suburbs has to follow the same pattern. Yes, a day spent walking around and across the tip of Manhattan offers an intriguing cross-section of time and place, but if the early history of New York intrigues you, you may want to spend a morning downtown exploring Trinity Church and its cemetery, then take the ferry to Staten Island to see historic Richmond Town, or the bus or subway uptown to see Gracie Mansion, an eighteenth-century country house that has survived in a surprising setting. Or you could follow up a morning's walk in any of several old neighborhoods with a visit to the Museum of the City of New York. Similarly, if you're enough of a museumgoer to manage more than one a day, you might choose to focus on a theme. For example, you can visit the Museum of Jewish Heritage downtown and the Jewish Museum uptown, or go from the elegance of the Morgan Library to the even more imposing elegance of the Frick Collection, or spend an afternoon at the Metropolitan Museum of Art, have an early dinner on the Upper East Side, then come back for a concert at the museum; getting concert tickets requires advance planning, of course, but, especially if it's one of the intimate concerts held in the museum's Temple of Dendur, it's an extremely civilized and memorable way to finish a day in New York.

Even for commuters, there's always the possibility of turning a work day into the opening act of a day trip—or, at any rate, an evening trip. The TKTS booths in Manhattan offer an excellent opportunity to purchase same-day theater tickets at half price, a great, spontaneous way to start a weekend. Similarly, an early dinner and a stroll through a museum on one of its late nights or a splurge on a concert or opera at Lincoln Center provides a nice punctuation mark in the midst of a routine workweek. The Metropolitan Museum of Art, for example, is open until 9 PM Fridays (and

Saturdays, too); the Whitney Museum of Art is also open until 9 PM on Fridays, and the Guggenheim is open until 8 PM both Friday and Saturday.

This book is meant to be a general resource for anyone who can, with reasonable convenience, get in a car or board a train or bus, reach the city, spend time there, and get home at a reasonable hour. It's for people with children and those without, people who like to wander by themselves and people who travel in groups, people who used to live in the city and those who never have, those who love cities and those who find them overwhelming.

■　　■　　■

For people like my husband and me, who grew up in New York and in the suburbs, this book may be a reminder of familiar favorites. For people who have recently moved to the area, it may be an introduction. People's lives change so much over the years that there's no one category that fits everyone all the time. Playgrounds and children's museums are so important, and then they aren't anymore. Quiet afternoons in museums and leisurely strolls along picturesque streets are so out of reach, and then suddenly they're not. The city itself changes, too. Places and activities that seem alien at one time may seem very inviting at another; destinations that seem too obvious at one stage may be just right five years later. The Lower East Side my grandmother left in the 1960s is the same Lower East Side that beckons my son and his friends now; the SoHo that seemed so distant and mysterious when I first started working in the city in the early 1970s is now a familiar stop on a high-schooler's shopping itinerary.

The constant is the magnitude and variety of New York City. This book only begins to touch on what the city as to offer, but I hope it will be just enough to tempt you to enjoy the places I've enjoyed, discover things that I haven't, and rediscover why you and millions of other people love New York.

1

The Tip of Manhattan:
The Beginning

■ ■ ■ ■ ■ ■ ■ ■ ■

AUTHOR'S NOTE: The tragic events of September 11, 2001, when terrorists attacked and destroyed the World Trade Center, changed lives and perceptions as well as the streetscape and skyline. As the first stages of the cleanup were completed and plans for the sixteen-acre World Trade Center site entered the discussion phase, it became clear that Lower Manhattan would be a work in progress for years to come. This chapter originally was written in late summer 2001 and completed the weekend before the attack. It was revised in late spring 2002. It may be years before the area physically returns to normal, and much longer than that before it feels the way it used to; perhaps it never will. It would be wrong to pretend that nothing happened and that this is a neighborhood like any other. All the same, it's an integral part of city history and city life, and there is a lot to see and do. This is still the oldest part of the city, the streets are still narrow and winding, the skyscrapers dramatic, the surviving small, old buildings fascinating and increasingly rare, and the atmosphere unlike that of newer, more orderly parts of the city.

Lower Manhattan is where New York began life as a city, decade by decade becoming a village, a town, a larger town, and finally a metropolis. The streets have evocative names, like streets in European cities. There are old, beautiful, and very historic churches, and equally historic graveyards. Here, at the relatively narrow tip of lower Manhattan, is one of the few places in the city where you can not only find a written record of what happened on a given spot three hundred years ago but also see buildings whose lives span at least two centuries. It's important to remember, too, that the place that became New York City was home to American Indians—the Lenapes—thousands of years before the Europeans arrived.

Only decades ago, lower Manhattan was silent on weekends, nearly empty of cars and people. Old brick buildings, two or three stories tall, looked like Edward Hopper paintings, when they didn't look like prints of pre–Civil War New York. There was a Horn and Hardart Automat on Park Row—one of those legendary, now-vanished self-service restaurants where you put money in a slot in the wall and took food out from behind a tiny glass door—and in summer it served iced cocoa. In those days, I used to accompany my father to his loft in an old building on Frankfort Street, where he made elegant brass and bronze lamps in classic urn designs. My grandmother sold them at her Third Avenue antiques shop, where they complemented her main offerings. My father had recently earned degrees in English under the GI Bill and had just become a high-school English teacher, so our trips downtown were a vanishing part of our family history, just as that version of lower Manhattan itself has mostly vanished.

Frankfort Street is still there, but the loft building and its similar neighbors are gone. The streets I remember from my early childhood are largely unrecognizable, altered by development in the 1960s and later. There is more recent, more drastic change too, of course, but Lower Manhattan remains a place to explore both the city's past and its present. In addition to offering a dazzling ambience and a good sampling of historic buildings, it is also the home of a diverse selection of excellent museums.

One way to start a trip to the tip of Manhattan is to spend some time walking on the beautifully landscaped **Esplanade** along the Hudson River, which runs from just north of the World Financial Center to Battery Park. The **World Financial Center** (www.worldfinancialcenter.com), completed in 1988, is the four-building commercial center of Battery Park City, which sits on a ninety-plus-acre site created by landfill, much of it from the massive excavation for the World Trade Center. The complex is south of Vesey Street and west of West Street. A pedestrian bridge—the fully enclosed North Bridge—once connected the WFC to the WTC, giving an impressive view of the crowds and bustle of West Street.

The most eye-catching aspect of the WFC was always the ten-story atrium known as the Winter Garden. It was destroyed on September 11 and was scheduled to reopen a year later. The original Winter Garden was just one component of the 300,000 square feet of public space in the WFC. With a circular marble staircase and a grove of palm trees, its interior was as striking as its Hudson River frontage. A spectacular orchid show was held each year, just one of dozens of exhibits, fairs, and performances—all free to the public—hosted by the WFC as part of its Arts and Events Program.

The waterside plaza in front of the complex still provides wonderful views of the water, and the restaurants and food shops began reopening in spring 2002. The North Cove Yacht Harbor, immediately south of the plaza, is worth a look. The World Financial Center Plaza—the entire Esplanade, in fact—is one of those places where Manhattan makes the most of the waterfront. After all, New York City has one of the world's great harbors. Two of the boroughs are self-contained islands; two more are part of a larger island; only the Bronx is attached to the mainland.

For visitors making the trip from the Erie Lackawanna Terminal in Hoboken, there's a spectacular way to get to lower Manhattan—NY Waterway's (800-533-3779; www.nywaterway.com) ferry service from the Hoboken Terminal to the World Financial Center, to Pier A at Battery Park, and to Pier 11 at Wall Street and the East River. The trip costs $3 and is part of the daily routine for many commuters, but that doesn't make it any less scenic. New York Waterway runs other commuter ferries as well, including routes from several additional New Jersey piers to the World Financial Center and other spots in lower Manhattan, as well as ferries to midtown (West 38th Street).

From the moment you leave the Hoboken rail terminal, the journey takes on a much more adventurous feeling than you get on a simple PATH ride or NJ Transit trip to Penn Station. The ornate, not-yet-renovated waterside of the terminal provides a backdrop to departure; it's weathered green like the Statue of Liberty. Once you are out on the river, you can see the George Washington Bridge to the far north and the Statue of Liberty and Ellis Island to the south. On the New Jersey side of the Hudson, the refurbished brick Central Railroad of New Jersey Terminal adds a nice touch. As you cross the river, on a slight diagonal toward the World Financial Center, you get the perfect tourist's-eye view of the Manhattan skyline, as well as a view of the Esplanade and other river traffic, including ferries, tugboats, New York City police boats, and the occasional pleasure craft.

Should the weather be cold or wet, you can travel in the ferry's indoor cabin if you prefer, but in good weather the open upper deck is what makes the trip special. It is somewhat noisy because this is not a sailboat, after all, but the visual delight more than makes up for the slight distraction of engine noise. In fact, if the weather is clear and you don't have time for the Staten Island Ferry, and you don't mind spending the $6 round-trip fare (keep in mind that the Staten Island Ferry is free but takes about half an hour each way), the Hoboken ferry trip is an excellent introduction to a day in the neighborhood.

If you are already in the city or are coming in to Penn Station or Grand Central, several subway routes will get you to Lower Manhattan. These include the Broadway-Seventh Avenue Local (1 and 9), the Eighth Avenue Express (A), and the versatile E train, whose L-shaped route curves from Sixth Avenue (Church Street) to Eighth Avenue to Queens.

A walk down along the river to Battery Park is a fine excursion in itself. As you wander down the Esplanade, you will find lots of benches for relaxing, reading, or enjoying the view of the river, the harbor, the Statue of Liberty, and the constantly changing Jersey City skyline across the river. Bikers and in-line skaters are allowed to use the lower part of the Esplanade closer to the water; the upper section is safer for slow walkers, small children, and people pushing strollers. The Esplanade and Battery Park City were heavily impacted by the terrorist attacks, but they have begun to revive. Battery Park City became an instant residential area when it was built, and continues to be visually delightful, with well-designed apartment buildings of varied height and style, playgrounds, lots of open space, and neighborhood shops along South End Avenue, the newly created main street that runs north-south one block inland from the Esplanade. From South End Avenue, short streets run at right angles to the park; the end of each street is highlighted by one of the fourteen pieces of "public art" that grace Battery Park City. My favorite is the open-air Greek temple with pebbly, reddish-brown columns.

One of the most spectacular stretches of the riverfront park is just north of the Museum of Jewish Heritage. The area is naturalized, with tall, graceful grasses punctuated by large rocks apparently brought in from elsewhere. There are wood trellises to provide both shade and visual interest, and a graceful curved stairway leads to a small viewing platform so you can admire the surroundings from above. A cove adds to the charm of the site. The museum's exterior is also distinctive—it is a square building with several layers of roofline rising in a pyramidlike shape above the main structure.

The **Museum of Jewish Heritage** (18 First Place, Battery Park City, 212-509-6130; www.mjhnyc.org) is a relatively recent addition to the city's major-museum collection, and it is worth a trip in its own right. Designed as a living memorial to the Holocaust, it is a riveting place that brings Jewish life of the past to present-day life. The museum focuses on the twentieth century, with extraordinarily evocative displays of photography, artwork, and artifacts. Personal narratives, including twenty-four films from Steven Spielberg's Survivors of the Shoah Visual History Foundation, are especially moving.

Although the fate of many of the people and places featured is grim, it is not a depressing museum, but a vibrant one, suitable for children as well as adults. I first visited it several years ago with my husband and our daughter, who was then about nine, and another family, whose children were about nine and twelve at the time. The girls didn't read the excellent descriptive material as carefully as the grownups, but there was certainly enough there—such as a 1945 picture of two smiling girls about their age who had recently been liberated from the concentration camp at Terezin—to engage their interest. We were especially moved by the displays that reminded us of the positive aspects of Jewish life in the past century and the richness of the culture.

Tickets are available at the museum box office or by calling 212-945-0039 or Ticketmaster, 800-307-4007. The museum is closed on Saturdays, Jewish holidays, and Thanksgiving Day. We were lucky enough to find on-street parking when we visited on a Sunday afternoon. You can also use public transportation: the M1, M6, M9, M10, and M15 buses all stop nearby. You can choose any of several subway stations: Whitehall Street for the N and R, Bowling Green for the 4 and 5; and Chambers Street for the A, C, and E. As I recall, we were especially lucky with parking that day. After the museum visit we drove to the Lower East Side for an early dinner at the **Second Avenue Deli** (156 Second Avenue at Tenth Street, 212-677-0606) and again both families found nearby on-street parking spaces.

Just south of the Museum of Jewish Heritage, a sign identifies the area as **Robert F. Wagner Jr. Park,** a beautifully landscaped area with rosebushes and other colorful seasonal plantings. On a visit there in August 2001, I found a listing (in both English and Latin) of every plant that was in bloom that week—multitudes of lilies, wild roses, and many others. It's an exhilarating example of good open-space planning at any time of year, though the wind can be piercing in winter.

The riverside walkway south of the museum is not quite as restful, and the park isn't as nice here as it is farther north—it is older, more heavily used, and more traditionally urban. It is very dynamic and surprisingly tourist-friendly, though. Informative signs posted by Heritage Trails New York and sponsored by several area financial and other institutions include maps, with pictures of selected attractions and a numerical key to the locations of many others.

One Heritage Trail billboard pointed me to **Pier A**, described as all that remains of a complex built for the Department of Docks and Harbor Police in 1886. In the midst of a renovation when I first saw it in August 2001, it was originally a place where important visitors were officially greeted. A clock added to the pier's tower in 1919 was the first permanent memorial to World War I servicemen. It was put to use as a commuter-ferry pier after September 11 and continues to serve as an additional ferry destination and departure point.

Just south of Pier A is the **American Merchant Marine**

Memorial. This dramatic monument by the sculptor Marisol is perched atop a rebuilt stone breakwater. Dedicated in 1991, it features four figures, two standing, one reaching down to help someone, and a final figure, not always visible, who represents a seaman struggling in the water. The fourth figure is, according to the plaque at water's edge, "submerged by each tidal cycle." When I walked past, only the figure's hand and forearm were above the water.

After you wind your way past these sites, you are within sight of **Battery Park,** once the area's major public green space; although it isn't as manicured and upscale in design as the newer park and esplanade that now lead to it, it does have a spectacular view and a lot of history behind it.

Battery Park is named for the battery of cannons that were meant to defend the city after the Revolution. The round brownstone building set back from the water is **Castle Clinton National Monument**. Built in the early 1800s as a fort to defend New York Harbor, it was used from 1855 to 1890 as an immigration center.

Even in mid-morning on a weekday in August, a month when the city is probably at its emptiest, Battery Park is teeming with people, tourists speaking many languages, vendors offering watches, hats, and miscellaneous souvenirs, bench-sitters, even a mime painted green and costumed to look like the Statue of Liberty. Tickets to Ellis Island and the Statue of Liberty are for sale at Castle Clinton, which serves as the National Park Service Visitor Center. There are lines to board the Ellis Island/Statue of Liberty ferries, and not a great deal of interpretive material at Castle Clinton (although rangers do give guided tours), but it's worth a walk around.

Away from the River

The tip of Manhattan is so full of history, historic places, and museums that you could probably spend a whole day there without taking time to see the riverfront. Where you go depends upon your own interests. The narrow streets and tall buildings, and the shade they cast, are legendary. That cliché of Wall Street's canyons has its basis in reality—the structures tower like cliffs over a narrow slice of street and sidewalk.

Signs along Battery Park's pathways point in various directions to other sights, large and small. Among the small ones are **New York Unearthed: City Archaeology**, a glass-covered archaeological dig on Pearl Street a few blocks up from Battery Park; here you can peek into an old cistern and see, in the shadow of a shiny, new, and very tall building, the remnants of the foundations of Governor Francis Lovelace's tavern. It only takes a minute or two to take in this particular site, but it's made more interesting by its location at the corner of Pearl Street and Coenties Slip/Coenties Alley. Pearl Street is narrow and perennially shaded, and Coenties Slip and Alley are even more picturesque; the Alley is for pedestrians only. The corner is a wonderful mix of bustle and peace, old and new, dark, narrow streets and glossy new development, tourists and people conducting their everyday lives. If you are thirsty and tired before you get there, you'll find a **Starbucks** at the corner of State and Pearl Street just across from Battery Park. On Pearl Street you may also find the Old Killarney, a bar whose sign and exterior suggest the Pearl Street of many decades ago.

Hanover Square is a tiny but refreshing open space at the intersection of Pearl, Hanover, Stone, and William Streets. It has benches where you can sit for a few minutes and contemplate the surroundings, especially the elegant brownstone building at 1 Hanover Square with the words "India House" carved across its front. Built in 1837, it became the first home of the Hanover Bank in 1851 and was transformed into a businessman's luncheon club in 1914. Nearby is another old building that's been put to good use. The **New York City Police Museum** (100 Old Slip, 212-480-3100) is located in a 1909 building that formerly housed the First Precinct. The museum is open weekdays from 10 AM to 5 PM.

Also on Pearl Street is the re-created **Fraunces Tavern** (54 Pearl Street), where George Washington made his farewell speech to his Revolutionary troops, on December 4, 1783. The restaurant (212-968-1776) on the ground floor of this cozy-looking brick building was recently renovated; there is a museum (212-425-1778) on the upper floors. Some of the exterior brick is from the original structure, which had already experienced a number of changes before it was purchased by the Sons of the Revolution in 1904 and was reconstructed shortly before World War I.

Relatively compact as the area is, there is a huge amount to see. For example, the signs in Battery Park also point to the **National Museum of the American Indian, George Gustav Heye Center** (1 Bowling Green, between State and Whitehall Streets, 212-514-3700;

www.si.edu.nmai), one of the newer reasons to visit lower Manhattan. The collection itself is the oldest of its kind in the United States; the building that houses it is the former United States Customs House, built in 1907. What's new is the placement of the collection at that particular site. The Museum of the American Indian was a quiet place in the 1980s, when I took my then school-age son to visit its former Audubon Terrace location in upper Manhattan. The exhibits were excellent, and we had the exhibit rooms almost to ourselves on that vacation weekday. The museum, now in a more heavily traveled and visited location, is being discovered and appreciated by many more people.

In 1989, Congress voted to create a National Museum of the American Indian as the sixteenth museum of the Smithsonian Institution. Its mission is to collaborate with native peoples of the Western Hemisphere to preserve their cultures. The cornerstone of the museum is the vast collection assembled by George Gustav Heye (1874–1957); the collection includes hundreds of thousands of items representative of all the major cultures of the Americas and ranging in age from Paleo-Indian to contemporary. The National Museum is made up of three facilities: the Heye Center in New York; a Cultural Resources Center in Suitland, Maryland; and a new, 260,000-square-foot museum in Washington, D.C., scheduled to open in 2004. At the Heye Center you can see selected items from the museum's holdings, which include Lakota robes, Kwakiutl wood carvings, Southwestern baskets, Navajo weavings, Central American ceramics, paintings and photographs reflecting travelers' views and images of Native American life, and a great deal more.

The building itself is also impressive. The exterior is massive and elaborate, with eye-catching columns and statues, and inside there is an amazing rotunda with an elliptical skylight. It's worth at least a peek inside even if you do not plan to explore the displays themselves. The museum is open daily from 10 AM to 5 PM and Thursday until 8 PM. It is closed December 25. Admission is free.

A few blocks uptown from the National Museum of the American Indian, past Bowling Green, is one of the longstanding stars of the neighborhood. **Trinity Church** (74 Trinity Place, 212-602-0800; www.trinitywallstreet.org), famously and perfectly juxtaposed against the corporate towers of the twentieth century, is a Gothic Revival structure dating to 1846. There has been a church on this site since the end of the seventeenth century, and thanks to its distinctive steeple, this particular Trinity Church was the tallest building in New York City for decades in the nineteenth century. It's very light and airy inside and has the intangible charm of old churches everywhere as well as the added interest of its place in New York City history. Even if you don't go inside, you'll have a picture-perfect moment gazing at the church and its tall spire.

Trinity Church is on the west side of Broadway just south of Wall Street and is open to the public daily, with tours each day at 2 PM. The church's museum features historical documents, maps, newspapers, burial records, photographs, and a variety of artifacts. Episcopal services are held daily and the church has an active congregation. Trinity Church sponsors a midday concert series of chamber and orchestral music on Mondays and Thursdays. A $2 donation is requested. For information, call 212-602-0747 or visit the Trinity Church Web site (www.trinitywallstreet.org). The church's original cemetery, on the north and south sides of the building, is almost disconcertingly peaceful, partly because it is unusual to find this much open green space in the immediate neighborhood. The parish's extensive history is reflected in some of the names on the monuments, which you may remember from history classes: William Bradford, who established the first printing press in what were then the colonies, is buried there. And so are Alexander Hamilton and Robert Fulton.

A few blocks farther north on Broadway, at Fulton Street, is **St. Paul's Chapel,** even older than Trinity Church and to me, even more elegant. Built in 1766, it is the oldest public building in continuous use in Manhattan. George Washington attended St. Paul's Chapel, and his pew is marked. It is a beautiful brownstone structure with a portico and elegant columns, modeled on St. Martin-in-the-Fields in London. There is a small, very atmospheric graveyard with eighteenth-century tombstones. The Chapel is part of Trinity Parish and is open daily from 9 AM to 3 PM and Sunday from 8 AM to 3 PM.

Since Lower Manhattan is the city's financial district, it's reasonable to expect some visitable sights that relate directly to the world of finance as well as the history and overall life of the city. Probably the most famous is the **New York Stock Exchange**. Before the September 11 attacks, tourists could visit its Interactive Education Center (20 Broad Street, 212-656-5168). At this writing, tours were no longer available. When they were (and perhaps they will be again, although when this book went to press there were no plans to reopen the Exchange to the public), free tickets were distributed outside the Broad Street entrance on a first-come, first-served basis. The visitor's gallery provided a view of the trading floor, and there were multilingual recorded explanations of the market's operations and a fifteen-minute video presentation to help visitors put what they were seeing into a larger perspective.

Wall Street continues to offers glimpses of distinctive architecture as well as history. **Federal Hall National Memorial** (26 Wall Street at Nassau Street, 212-825-6888; www.nps.gov/feha) is a massive Greek Revival building modeled on the Parthenon. It was built in 1842 and originally served as a custom house, and it occupies the site on which George Washington was sworn in as president of the United States in 1789. There's a statue of him on the steps of the building. Admission to the interior, which contains an impressive rotunda and various historical exhibits, is free; it is open weekdays from 9 AM to 5 PM and is closed on weekends and on federal holidays.

The New York Stock Exchange

The East River

There is an East River Esplanade; it isn't as elegant as the one along the Hudson, but it does provide great views of Brooklyn Heights. You can walk all the way here along the waterfront, or cut over on Fulton Street from the World Trade Center site to get to South Street Seaport, one of the multi-faceted attractions of the eastern side of lowest Manhattan. You can also get here via public transportation, such as the M15 bus down Second Avenue or any one of several subways—the 2, J, Z, or M to Fulton Street or the 4, 5, A, or C to Broadway-Nassau. In each case, you then walk east on Fulton Street to the Seaport.

If seafaring and New York's history as a port interest you, or if you have children intrigued by the romance of the seafaring life, **South Seaport and Museum** (Water and South Streets, 212-748-8600 or 212-SEA-PORT/732-7678; www.southstseaport.org and www.southstreetseaport.com) could be the major destination of your trip to lower Manhattan. Or you could stop in briefly to shop, eat lunch, or gaze at the boats docked in the East River. The fact that the Seaport has two telephone numbers and two Web address tells you something about its split identity.

The area once was the heart of a bustling waterfront. Sailing ships docked off South Street; chandleries, sailor's hotels, and other maritime businesses were concentrated along Fulton and neighboring streets. The museum was founded in 1967 with the goal of preserving both buildings and ships during a period when lower Manhattan's historic fabric was threatened by both construction of new buildings and removal of old ones for parking areas. The South Street Seaport Historic District was designated in 1977.

Part of South Street Seaport is a monument to life aboard ship over the past century or more; part of it is a historical museum; and part of it, with no apologies, is a mall. To some visitors, the best thing about South Street Seaport may be the beautiful old buildings, whose survival is one of the great success stories of the preservation movement. To others, the thrill will be the wonderful boats, especially the *Peking* and the *Wavertree*. And to inveterate shoppers, the area's greatest appeal may be in the many shops of Pier 17, an indoor mall, and the refurbished blocks adjacent to the Seaport, where Gap and J. Crew and other retailers sell familiar wares.

When I was a child, there were fishing boats from Gloucester and New Bedford at the docks, and no tourists. Where those fishing boats used to dock is now the waterfront part of South Street Seaport. There is a wonderful wide wooden dock here, and pulled up against Pier 16 are the various ships and boats, some of them National Historic Landmarks in their own right, that are one of the hearts of the Seaport. The tall ships form a graceful, dramatic skyline of their own along the waterfront, though small compared to the buildings of the Financial District that loom behind them. You need to buy an admission ticket to the museum in order to board the ships, though admiring them from the dock is free. The museum is open daily from May to September and daily except Tuesday October through April.

The view of the four-masted barque *Peking,* built in 1911, is especially dramatic. The rigging, restored in the mid-1990s, is elegant, and with the tallest of its masts measuring 170 feet in height, it towers over the older buildings of the Seaport, just as the skyscrapers slightly inland tower over it. The museum purchased the *Peking* in 1975, and it is the largest sailing ship preserved as a museum, and one of the largest sailing ships ever built. The *Wavertree,* built in 1885, was one of the last sailing ships built of wrought iron. She had a rather sad life and was dismasted off Cape Horn early in the twentieth century. Later she was used as a floating warehouse in Chile and as a sand barge in Argentina. The Seaport acquired *Wavertree* in 1968, and in the summer of 2001 she was being restored to her appearance as a sailing ship. *Ambrose* is chunkier, looking like a basic tugboat at first careless glance, but it is in fact a lightship, built in 1908 to guide ships from the Atlantic into lower New York Bay. The water was too deep and the bottom too soft to allow for a lighthouse, so the lightship was used as a warning beacon. The Coast Guard gave the *Ambrose* to the museum in 1968, and it now houses photographs, charts, and artifacts about lightships and navigation.

If the sight of the historic vessels at dockside make you want to get out on the water, South Street offers that opportunity as well. The 1930 tugboat *W. O. Decker* cruises New York Harbor on Saturdays from April to October; itineraries and times vary. The 1885 schooner *Pioneer* also offers regularly scheduled public sails from Memorial Day through Labor Day. These go to Roosevelt Island in the East River, now the site of a large planned residential community, formerly used as an isolation hospital and prison and known as Blackwell's Island. NY Waterway also has an outpost at Pier 17 and offers harbor cruises from that location.

The ambience of Pier 17 is in marked contrast to the historic seafaring mood and experience of Pier 16. It was built as a shopping and eating space,

and once you step inside it has the familiar mall feeling. It also has spectacular views of the waterfront, the ships, and the East River bridges from
balconies adjacent to the indoor shopping areas. On a hot August day, the
view of the Brooklyn Bridge from one of the north-facing balconies was
almost breathtaking; unfortunately, overflowing dumpsters below the balcony
apparently contained several days' worth of summer-simmered garbage. In
addition to a good but not unique mix of chain and souvenir shops, Pier 17
has a nicely varied food court and large, clean, easy-to-find rest rooms.

As you leave Pier 17 and head west to Fulton Street, you'll realize there
is still a Fulton Fish Market at the base of Fulton Street, along South Street,
near where Fulton Street once met the East River (although in summer 2002
plans were announced to move the fish market to Hunts Point in the Bronx
in 2004). It's an early-morning place, and a less overwhelming presence than
it was even half a century ago, but you can still see signs along South Street
announcing a number of firms selling fish, lobster, and shrimp to retailers.
Along Fulton Street, the commercial bustle is more contemporary, with a
cobbled pedestrian area and the Fulton Market Building combining a bit of
fish-market history with a new set of retailers. The beautifully restored brick
buildings on Front Street north of Fulton Street house modern stores. The
buildings of Schermerhorn Row, running along the South Side of Fulton
Street, are the nucleus of the district. Completed in 1812, they originally
housed a variety of businesses. These landmarks were built in a Georgian
Federal style; in the 1840s, some of the brick fronts were replaced by granite-
piered Greek Revival fronts, and later in the century some were again updated
with cast-iron columns—like the ones that make SoHo so distinctive.
Although the shop fronts were changed, the upper floors and the rooflines are
close to their original appearance. Some of the interior upper-floor spaces,
some of which were used as lodging houses, were also unchanged until very
recently. They are part of the space to be opened to the public when the
museum inaugurates its major permanent exhibit in 2003: the "World Port
New York," to be housed on the upper floors of the Schermerhorn Row and
the A. A. Low building, which backs onto the Row.

Walking west on Fulton Street, you will find there is actually a small
hill, making it easy to imagine a sloping hillside that once ran down to a
bustling waterfront. Heading up Fulton Street on a weekday plunges you
into crowds of people on their way to or from work, meetings, and business
errands. One pleasant stopping point is the **Strand Book Store Annex**

(95 Fulton Street, 212-732-6070). The main Strand Book Store, a legendary emporium for used and antiquarian books, is a bit farther uptown, at Broadway and Twelfth Street. Even the Annex is huge, however, and though I was there on a very warm day and the store was not air-conditioned, I had a great time browsing the countless aisles and shelves and tables of books, from cookbooks to readable light fiction to specialized history, and more.

Stumbling upon the downtown Annex was a nice surprise toward the end of my long walk around Lower Manhattan. Another unexpected treat, a much smaller one, was the Asian man who was making intricate origami-like animals and insects out of dried reeds and grasses. He was working at a tiny table and had dozens of samples on display, ranging from butterflies for $7 (which I couldn't resist buying) to even more impressive snakes and crickets for about $20. You may not find the same craftsperson as you walk through the city, but there is always the possibility of discovering an equally interesting and appealing scene in the midst of mainstream bustle.

There's a complex set of subway stations at Fulton Street, Wall Street, Nassau Street, and Broadway; from Broadway/Nassau the 4 and 5 trains will take you to Grand Central, and the A and C will take you to Penn Station; the 2 train from Fulton or Wall Streets also takes you to Penn Station. Check the signs above the station entrances to be sure you're descending toward the right line for your next destination. You can also take one of several buses uptown if you'd prefer a more scenic though slower ride.

2

Lower Manhattan East:
A Little of Almost Everything

One of my favorite recent New York City excursions took place on a chilly Sunday in November, when I spent several hours walking with a group of strangers through one of the traditionally least glamorous parts of Manhattan, the once predominantly Jewish Lower East Side, the area bounded by the East River on the east, Canal Street on the south, 14th Street on the north, and the Bowery on the west. At various times during the past century and a half, diverse immigrant groups have inhabited different sections of this area. That continues to be the case; there is a large Chinese-speaking population in the southern section, many Spanish-speaking people farther north, and throughout the neighborhood, there are pockets of increasing affluence, populated by prosperous descendants of earlier immigrants. The walking tour I joined covered a relatively limited route, from Canal Street at East Broadway up Essex Street, ending at Houston Street. It was one of many walking tours listed in the Weekend section of the Friday *New York Times;* there are usually at least several reasonably priced tours listed, sponsored by a variety of groups, and they explore neighborhoods, vanished lifestyles, even cemeteries, throughout the city. They are typically scheduled for Saturday or Sunday afternoons, but there are occasional weekday tours. Some require advance reservations and don't publish their departure points; others are more casual and you can just show up and pay the fee at the specified meeting place. The one I took was offered by **Joyce Gold History Tours of New York** (212-242-5762; www.nyctours.com) and didn't require advance reservations.

The tour started at Straus Square, a little plaza that is more than a sidewalk, less than a vest-pocket park, in the shadow of the old **Forward Building** (175 East Broadway). The *Forward* was the Yiddish daily newspaper that my grandmother and many others of her generation and background read. (It is still published—now in both Yiddish and English—but not from its original quarters.) I reached the meeting place by walking east almost the entire length of Canal Street from the C train subway station near the entrance to the Holland Tunnel—I had taken NJ Transit to Penn Station and connected with the subway from there. After passing vendors' stalls selling presumably counterfeit Prada and Kate Spade bags and backpacks, I crossed the street to be tempted by snacks, pastries, and colorful fruit drinks at Chinese restaurants and bakeries. Across Broadway, street life seemed a little more subdued, and I finally reached Straus Square on a quiet part of Canal Street at East Broadway. Two other walking tours were also using that little plaza as a rendezvous point. There was a sense of shared adventure as people from assorted neighborhoods, cities, and even countries began to gather.

As we left on the start of our trip, Joyce Gold, who specializes in local history and has been leading walking tours for decades, pointed out a building under renovation near the East Broadway station of the F train and noted that apartments in the building, within walking distance to the Financial District, would be renting for about $2,000 a month. Members of the tour included a German tourist, a couple from New Orleans visiting their daughter who had recently moved to the city, and an elderly woman who remembered the neighborhood from the days before World War II, when its original immigrant population was still a strong presence. Gold pointed out a variety of interesting sites, including the impressive **St. Theresa's Church** (16/18 Rutgers Street), which was built as a Presbyterian church in 1841 but has served as a Catholic church since 1863, reflecting the changing neighborhood population. Another highlight was the **Educational Alliance** (197 East Broadway, 212-780-2300), a Romanesque Revival building dating to 1889. Originally known as the Hebrew Institute, the Educational Alliance offered English classes to immigrants and housed a free library, the only one in the city at that time. The Educational Alliance is still a neighborhood cultural center, one of several settlement houses founded by more affluent, longer established German Jews to help recent Eastern European immigrants in the late nineteenth century. Just across the street is the **Seward Park Library** (192 East Broadway), built in 1909; it has a rooftop garden to provide an outdoor reading area in a neighborhood where outdoor space is severely limited. We also saw several old synagogues that had been converted to other uses, as well as the Eldridge Street Synagogue, several food shops, including the famous Guss Pickles on Essex Street, where many tour members got in line to buy plastic tubs of cucumbers in varying stages of pickling. Being part of a group, and such a varied one, added to the fun of rediscovery and probably led me to several places I would not have found on my own.

> Although I deliberately used a route that would give me the opportunity to take an exploratory walk before the official tour, you can get much closer to the heart of this neighborhood by talking the F train to the East Broadway station, which is the last downtown stop in Manhattan before the train continues to Brooklyn.

Whether you join a walking tour or decide to explore on your own, the Lower East Side may surprise you. It's varied and vibrant, and though parts of it may still look rundown and off-putting to the suburban eye, it's definitely worth a visit.

One of the star attractions of the neighborhood is the **Lower East Side Tenement Museum** (90 Orchard Street and 97 Orchard Street, 212-431-0233; www.tenement.org). For those of us who grew up with *Little House on the Prairie*—the books or the television series—it is nice to be reminded that not all pioneering families lived in the sparsely settled western reaches of the United States. There's a great deal of American history on city streets, too, and the Tenement Museum does a wonderful job of bringing it to life. The heart of the museum experience is the restored building at 97 Orchard Street, where visitors are taken on a tour of several re-created apartments reflecting several eras and ethnic backgrounds. At the visitor center across the street, you'll find excellent photographs and other exhibits that provide further insight into immigrant life in the late nineteenth and early twentieth centuries. The gallery is free, but you do need to purchase tickets for the tours, and the number of people on each tour is limited. You can buy tickets for the tenement tour, the Confino apartment program, and walking tours on the day of your visit at the visitor center. Tickets for the tenement tours and the special Confino apartment tours can be purchased at least one day ahead of time from TicketWeb (800-965-4827; www.ticketweb.com).

The regular tenement tour takes about one and a quarter hours. You see three apartments, one reflecting the life of a German-Jewish dressmaker in the nineteenth century, one illustrating the life of a Sicilian family in the 1930s, and one featuring a Russian-Jewish family in 1918. Tickets cost $9 for adults, $7 for students and senior citizens. A special living-history tour designed especially for families with children is offered several times a day on weekends. Tickets cost $8 for adults, $6 for students and senior citizens. This forty-five-minute tour takes you to the Confino apartment, where a costumed interpreter explains the lives of a newly arrived Sephardic Jewish family from Greece about 1916. Visitors are allowed to touch items in this apartment and to try on period clothing. On weekends April through December, the museum also offers a walking tour of the Lower East Side called "Streets Where We Lived." The ticket price is $9 for adults, $7 for students and senior citizens.

The first time I tried to visit the museum on a Sunday afternoon there were no tickets available for the next tenement tour, so I just spent time at the exhibit gallery; the next time, I came during the week to be sure to get in. If you want to be sure of making a specific tour, it might be worth paying the TicketWeb service fee for advance tickets. The museum is open from noon to 5 PM Tuesday through Friday and from 11 AM to 5 PM on weekends. If you grew up in a small city apartment, or as a child visited a grandparent or other relative in that kind of apartment, you will feel especially nostalgic when you see the tiny rooms, simple furnishings, and hints of everyday life. But even if you grew up on a farm or visited your grandparents in a colonial mansion, a visit to the Tenement Museum is a fascinating trip to an important part of the American experience.

The **Eldridge Street Synagogue** (12 Eldridge Street, 212-291-0903; www.eldridgestreet.org) is another treasure of this neighborhood, not just for religious reasons but because it is an impressive and beautiful building with an interesting story. I had known about it for years, but I had never seen it in person until I took the Joyce Gold tour, which gave me a chance to see the exterior.

This very decorative building, also known as Congregation K'hal Adath Jeshurun and Anshe Lubz, combines several styles—Gothic, Romanesque, and, especially, Moorish—in its elaborate facade; it is a city landmark and a National Historic Landmark and is on the National Register of Historic Places. Completed in 1887 for the first congregation of Eastern European Orthodox Jews in the country, it was once the largest Jewish house of worship in the neighborhood. It is tucked away on a busy but surprisingly narrow street lined with tenements and low buildings housing small businesses; some have stoops in front, a streetscape somehow familiar but not quite of this era. The Jewish population of the neighborhood declined dramatically by the middle of the twentieth century and the congregation grew much smaller, leading to years of neglect. Restoration and preservation efforts are ongoing, under the auspices of the Eldridge Street Project, a not-for-profit cultural organization. The synagogue's interior is noted for its woodwork and chandeliers and is open for tours on Tuesdays, Thursdays, and Sundays; call for times and fees. In addition, the synagogue continues to serve its congregation, as it has been for more than 110 years, with Sabbath and holiday services.

Cultural and historic considerations aside, you may want to spend an hour or two—more if you are a real shopper—exploring the stores on **Orchard Street** and its environs, including Grand, Ludlow, and Broome Streets. It is heavily promoted by the Lower East Side Business Improvement District, a nonprofit economic-development organization. The BID visitor center at 261 Broome Street (212-226-9010, 888-VALUES-4/825-8374; www.lowereastsideny.com) is open Monday through Friday and Sunday from 10 AM to 4 PM, and there is a free parking lot on Broome Street between Norfolk and Suffolk Streets. Like many of the businesses in the neighborhood, it is closed on Saturday, the Jewish Sabbath. The neighborhood is especially known for clothing and accessory boutiques and fabric and home-furnishings stores. The combination of distinctive urban ambience, name brands, and the perception of bargain prices sets it apart from other shopping districts. Among the best-known of the too-many-to name shopping finds are **Forman's** (80, 82, and 84 Orchard Street, 212-777-3600) and **Fine & Klein** (119 Orchard Street, 212- 674-6720).

Food is the companion piece to the traditional bargain/fashion shopping in the area bounded roughly by Houston Street on the north, Suffolk Street on the east, Canal Street on the south, and Forsyth Street on the west. It is still home to many shops that sell traditional Jewish and Eastern European foods, so it offers nostalgia as well as good eating. For many visitors, they are places to get good food, as Chinatown and Little Italy are to me. For others, including me, the shops also bring back the smells and tastes and accents of my early childhood, when I visited my grandmother in what is now Alphabet City—the numbered streets and letter-name avenues on the far east side of Manhattan between Houston Street and 14th Street. Shopping for food for her family was important to my grandmother, and she used to take me with her to bakeries and shops along Avenue C to buy rye bread and onion rolls, whitefish and pickles. In those days, there were still some push-carts where she bought fruits and vegetables, and the conversations and transactions were largely in Yiddish, with a little heavily inflected English here and there. My grandmother's generation is gone now, and Avenue C has changed ethnicity and style several times since the 1950s, but the ghost of the experience is still to be found farther down the East Side, where the wide cross streets feed into East River bridges and people from the suburbs and more affluent neighborhoods uptown come to revisit their past. Several of the shops are both well known and, in a way, fashionable. **Russ & Daughters** (179 East Houston Street, 212-475-4880; www.russanddaughters.com) is a long-time purveyor of smoked fish and related delicacies. Nearby, one of my perennial favorites is **Moishe's Homemade Kosher Bakery** (East 181 Houston Street, 212-475-9624). When I lived in the city in the 1970s, I used to walk down to Houston Street from my apartment in the East 20s to buy Russian rye bread with black caraway seeds; later my husband and I would make the trip together for wonderfully fragrant loaves of what he called corn bread—not cornbread in the American sense but sturdy rye bread. On our Sunday excursions we also used to stop at **Yonah Schimmel's Knishes** (137 East Houston Street, 212-477-2858; www.yonahschimmel.com), where you can buy knishes to either take home or enjoy on the spot. Established in 1919, Yonah Schimmel is a legendary spot, with tin ceilings and an unadorned storefront. In addition to standbys like potato knishes and kasha knishes, you can get a number of other fillings, such as cabbage, and also discover surprisingly light sweet cheese knishes. A few blocks south and east, the **Essex Street Market** (120 Essex Street, north of Delancey) is now an old-fashioned covered market, with many stalls offering not only food but also clothes and other items. When it was created decades ago by Mayor Fiorello LaGuardia, it was a modern market designed to bring the neighborhood's pushcarts inside and under one roof. The Essex Street Market is open Monday through Saturday, closed Sundays. Across the street from the market, follow your nose or other enthusiastic customers to **Guss Pickles** (35 Essex Street, 800-252-4877; www.gusspickles.com). I have always thought that puckeringly sour pickles were the only real choice in the pickle world, but people with tamer tastes may enjoy half-sour pickles, and adventurous types will want to branch out to such specialties as pickled green tomatoes. Guss has them all, and more. (At this writing, Guss Pickles was moving from its Essex Street quarters; call for its present location.)

Katz's Delicatessen (205 East Houston Street, 212-254-2246) is another classic neighborhood food stop. It opened in 1888 and is still one of those places you are supposed to visit to complete the New York experience. It specializes in classics like pastrami sandwiches, beef salami, and kosher frankfurters (although Katz's is not a kosher restaurant, just one that serves Eastern European Jewish–style food). It isn't fancy, but it is very good. Even better, though much more expensive, since it's a place to go for dinner, is **Sammy's Roumanian Steak House** (157 Chrystie Street, 212-673-0330). The first time I ate there was a Saturday in December 1975. It serves lots of meat, notably rib steak and other cuts of beef, and appropriate accompaniments like mashed potatoes with little fried bits of onions and gribenes (cracklings). Like Katz's, it is not kosher, but it is very ethnic, and wonderful. For my family, the food and the old-fashioned seltzer bottles and Fox's U-Bet syrup were reminders of childhood treats. The thing that stays in my memory most about my first meal at Sammy's is that after an early dinner we walked up to Madison Square Garden to watch a Knicks game, never felt cold at any point on the walk, and still felt as though we had just eaten by the time we got to our seats high above the Garden floor.

Orchard Street is known for its shops and active street life, so getting there on your own should not present a problem. You can take the M15 bus down Second Avenue, which becomes Forsyth Street south of Houston Street; get off at Delancey Street and walk east to Orchard Street and then one block north to the Tenement Museum if that's on your itinerary. Coming from downtown, the M15 bus will also work; its route starts all the way down at the Staten Island Ferry Terminal. You can also take the subway: the F train stops at Delancey Street.

Immersed as it is in history, the Lower East Side has a new identity, too, as a place where the arts flourish and twenty-somethings hang out. There are fashionable new shops, restaurants, and clubs on Clinton Street, Ludlow Street, Stanton Street, and the others in the grid of named streets below Houston. The trouble with being fashionable, of course, is that the names and addresses that are current as I write may not be the ones that dazzle when you read this a year or two later. In 2001, one of the best-known of the sophisticated new restaurants was **71 Clinton Fresh Food** (71 Clinton Street, between Stanton and Rivington Streets, 212-614-6960), open for dinner only.

As they have gentrified in the past decade, the streets of the Lower East Side, not only below Houston Street but also farther uptown in Alphabet City—named for its Avenues A, B, C, and D east of First Avenue—have changed markedly. On a recent ride on the M15 bus up from Wall Street along Allen Street (which becomes First Avenue above Houston Street), I noticed a young woman relaxing on a deck chair in the early autumn sunshine on the second-floor terrace of a pink stucco apartment building at the corner of Houston Street—a Miami-meets-Westchester moment. It wasn't my grandmother's Lower East Side, but it was alive and clean and even welcoming again.

I left the bus at 8th Street to explore Tompkins Square Park, which for years was not a place where you would necessarily want to sit and read, or even walk. It occupies the blocks from 10th Street to 7th Street between Avenue A and Avenue B, and as I walked up Avenue A to the northern edge of the park I was struck by how pretty it is, and how neatly renovated the buildings facing the park on 10th Street are. Most were not tenements at all, but brownstone-style town houses, not very different from the ones you might expect to see in Greenwich Village or on the Upper West Side. Although the western part of the park was almost deserted, the paths and benches in the section nearest Avenue B were well populated. On an impulse I decided to walk farther east to 7th Street and Avenue D, where my mother grew up and where my grandmother continued to live until the early 1960s. Avenue B was narrow and almost quaint, enlivened by a variety of storefronts and restaurants. Almost every building on 7th Street had been renovated or was in the midst of renovation. The sidewalks were clean, people of all ages and ethnic groups were working on the buildings or chatting at the entryways, and throughout the neighborhood there was a mix of old and new residents, shops, and eateries.

If you have family roots in the area or are interested in exploring emerging neighborhoods, it's an interesting destination, and once you get back to First and Second Avenues, you are in a long-standing Eastern European neighborhood known for established restaurants and shops. I had lunch at **Veselka** (144 Second Avenue at 9th Street, 212-228-9682), a Ukrainian restaurant that has been around for a long time but feels very contemporary, partly because it has exposed brick walls and partly because many of the customers, at least the afternoon I was there, look and sound like drama students. (Quite possibly they are, since NYU is only a few blocks away and has both graduate and undergraduate theater programs.) Veselka's menu features a number of dishes that would be familiar to anyone whose grandmother grew up east of the Elbe. My cup of cold borscht was good as well as nostalgic, and my vegetarian paté plate was delicious. (Vegetarian paté is basically fake chopped liver, made with green beans, hard-boiled eggs, and fried onions; it sounds odd but it can be really good.) The legendary—and kosher—**Second Avenue Deli** (156 Second Avenue, 212-677-0606) is just a block downtown. There are also a number of Ukrainian and Polish restaurants on the surrounding blocks, as well as a tempting variety of other ethnic restaurants, such as **Holy Basil** (149 Second Avenue, 212-460-5557), a popular Thai restaurant. Directly across Second Avenue from Veselka are two newcomers that seal the neighborhood's identity as up-and-coming mainstream: a Starbucks and a Burritoville; traditionalists will be happy to notice that J. Baczynsky's meat market is still on that block, a survivor from an earlier time. Interestingly, if you walk up First Avenue just a few blocks, you switch European zones quickly and come upon two well-known Italian café/pastry shops, **Veniero's Pasticceria** (342 11th Street, just west of First Avenue, 212-674-7264) and **De Robertis Pasticceria** (176 First Avenue, between 10th and 11th Streets, 212-674-7137).

Second Avenue at 10th Street represents an intriguing point of intersection of several worlds: the Lower East Side, with its immigrant past and present overlapping its gentrified present and probable future; St. Mark's Place (8th Street between Second and Third Avenue), seedy now but glamorous once in its heyday as a center of 1960s youth culture; and a relic of a much earlier New York—the elegant brownstones of Stuyvesant Street adjacent to St. Mark's-in-the-Bowery, one of the most beautiful churches in the city. **Stuyvesant Street,** between Second and Third Avenues and 9th and 10th Streets, is an anomaly in this part of Manhattan—a street that appears to run diagonally within the normal rectangular street grid (although in fact it runs exactly east-west; it is the rest of the grid that veers off the compass). Named for Peter Stuyvesant, whose farm (*bouwerie*) once occupied this area, it's a lovely street, lined with nineteenth-century brick and brownstone row houses. **St. Mark's-in-the-Bowery** (131 East 10th Street, 212-674-6377), at the east end of the street, looks very unlike a big-city house of worship and very like a perfect eighteenth-century country church. Built in 1799, it was once a country church, when the area consisted of farmland, and its fieldstone exterior continues to give it a rustic look.

When Downtown Was Uptown

St. Mark's-in-the-Bowery gives a hint of the neighborhood's eighteenth-century life. A few blocks west and south, there's another rather elegant reminder of early New York. The **Merchant's House Museum** (29 East 4th Street, 212-277-1089; www.merchantshouse.com) is a slightly faded-looking brick town house on a nondescript block just west of the Bowery. When it was built in 1832, it was part of an affluent neighborhood of row houses populated largely by wealthy merchants who had moved uptown from the tip of Manhattan. A merchant named Seabury Tredwell moved into the house in 1835; one of his daughters, Gertrude Tredwell, was born in the house in 1840 and lived there all her life; she died in the house in 1933. By then the neighborhood had again changed identity, becoming partly industrial and not at all elegant. The house had survived virtually unchanged for nearly a century and remains a wonderful record of how prosperous people lived in style and comfort in nineteenth-century New York City. The Seabury Tredwell House, as it was then known, was documented by the Historic American Buildings Survey in 1936 and became a museum that same year. It is a National Historic Landmark as well as a New York City Landmark and is listed on the National Register of Historic Places. The museum is a member of the Historic House Trust of New York City, a not-for-profit organization that works with the City of New York Department of Parks and Recreation to preserve a number of historic houses in the city.

The house has relatively limited hours; it is open Thursday through Monday from 1 PM to 5 PM. Weekday tours are self-guided, supported by a detailed, informative booklet that you borrow from the museum office/gift shop. On weekends, guided tours are available. I enjoyed my self-guided tour on a Friday afternoon and was a little surprised not to have the house entirely to myself; other visitors included two Swedish couples who had stopped by the house as part of their trip to New York City. Though not a major attraction, the house does make an interesting stopover if you are in the neighborhood; it is also a good footnote to a visit to South Street Seaport, the area where Seabury Tredwell made his money and from which he moved his family home in 1835. If you have time to take the M15 bus up from South Street to First Avenue and East Fourth Street, then walk west to the museum, you will have a slow but enlightening view of a series of New York City areas, from the eastern edges of Chinatown up through the Lower East Side.

Chinatown and Little Italy

New York has always been a city of immigrants, and it's the neighborhoods most closely associated with immigrant life that give New York much of its novelty. For many of us, these neighborhoods are part of family history; for others of us, they represent the opportunity to explore another culture without going very far from home. Manhattan's Chinatown has expanded tremendously in recent decades, and Little Italy has shrunk somewhat. Whatever your own ethnicity, both areas are good destinations for strolling, shopping, and eating. Its borders have expanded considerably north and east, but the most familiar part of Chinatown, with a wealth of restaurants, snack shops, bakeries, supermarkets, and specialty shops, runs along Canal Street and south of Canal Street along streets such as Pell, Bayard, Doyers, and Baxter. There's also a museum that should appeal to anyone with an interest in city history, Chinese-American culture, and immigration in general. The **Museum of Chinese in America** (70 Mulberry Street at Bayard Street, 212-619-4785; www.moca-nyc.org), located in a former school building, enlightens visitors about the Chinese-American experience. Its permanent exhibit, "Where's Home? Chinese in the Americas," displays artifacts as varied as Chinese musical instruments, old shop signs, and domestic items.

Neighboring Little Italy centers on Mulberry, Mott, and Elizabeth Streets north of Canal, running east to the Bowery and north to Kenmare. Decades ago, a friend of my parents used to bring us Italian pastries from **Ferrara's** (195 Grand Street, between Mott and Mulberry Streets, 212-226-6150); certainly there are other pastry shops and specialty food stores to enliven a walk in Little Italy, but it's Ferrara's that has stayed with me as a delicious symbol of the neighborhood. On the northern fringes, above Spring Street, the area now known as NoLita (North of Little Italy) merges almost imperceptibly into SoHo, albeit with its own of-the-moment blend of boutiques and restaurants.

3

SoHo:
Not Just Art Galleries

In the early 1980s, when I worked on Greene Street for a tiny branch office of the company that publishes *Better Homes and Gardens,* SoHo was in its early prime. It was no longer exactly avant-garde: the lofts had become fashionable, not just as workplaces for struggling artists but as homes for the affluent who wanted to maintain a bit of unconventionality. Trucks lined the streets, and the sidewalks were often cluttered with boxes, but the upscale grocer Dean and DeLuca was already there, along with an assortment of sophisticated home-goods stores, and the first generation of very good restaurants. And of course there was then, as there had been long before and continues to be, **Fanelli's,** a classic bar on Prince Street near Mercer (212-431-5744).

Although in my commuting days I liked walking past the cast-iron buildings that gave SoHo its identity and that had inspired a group of dedicated preservationists to save the neighborhood from a Robert Moses–inspired Lower Manhattan Expressway in the early 1960s, I didn't usually have time to appreciate the buildings. Occasionally at lunchtime, though, I did walk around, especially enjoying the trompe-l'oeil painting of windows and cats on the plain east-facing wall of a building off Prince Street. I used to gaze at the wall as I ate at Food, at the corner of Prince and Wooster Street. It was a glorified cafeteria, a self-service place with carefully prepared food—with an emphasis on creative vegetarian main courses, heavily bean sprouted salads, good bread, and very good desserts.

That wasn't my first job in the neighborhood; in the mid-1970s I worked on its southwestern fringes, at the corner of Sixth Avenue and Spring Street, editing crafts books for Butterick, a company better known for its sewing patterns but which once published a wonderful women's magazine called *The Delineator*. One appealing aspect of the job was being able to walk east a block or two along Spring Street and splurge on lunch at the SoHo Charcuterie. Quiche was fashionable then, and interesting salads still a novelty. A small store on the south side of Spring Street was introducing an exotic new line of Vermont-made ice creams in carefully selected flavors—early Ben and Jerry's.

Butterick moved to midtown, the SoHo Charcuterie is long gone, everyone knows about Ben and Jerry's now, and Food has disappeared from its Prince Street corner, replaced by a clothing store. But SoHo remains a delight for walkers, shoppers, and admirers of city life, whether on their lunch hours or visiting from the leafier realms of suburbia. The streets are lined with places to look, admire, long for, and maybe buy everything from works of art to bath salts to architectural salvage items to clothes.

I discovered SoHo's new identity a couple of summers ago when the mother of one of my daughter's friends suggested that the four of us go into the city for a day of wandering and shopping. We walked from the Christopher Street PATH station and made our first stop at a below-ground-level treasure trove called **girlprops.com** (153 Prince Street, 212-505-7615; www.girlprops.com). It has a zebra-striped entrance and a vibrant interior full of colorful, glittery temptations. The store's motto is "Inexpensive—we never say cheap," and given the abundance of items priced under $10, I'd say that was a more than fair assessment. I'd call it cheap in a good way, but I'll respect the store's preference and say it's wonderfully inexpensive. The girls were entranced by the glitter and left, happily, with barrettes, decorative sunglasses, and brightly beaded necklaces.

It's true that SoHo is still a place of galleries, a place where you can contemplate contemporary art as well as more traditional works, or spot a fashionable-looking man, dressed all in black, speaking French into a tiny cell phone while apparently overseeing deliveries at a store that looks even more fashionable than he does. But it's also very much a place where high-school girls can buy Todd Oldham jeans at the source. Of course those jeans, along with lots of other brands a (price) step beyond Gap Classics, are available in stores in Millburn, Mt. Kisco, and dozens of suburb towns, but it's much more fun to go into the spacious, airy **Todd Oldham** boutique (123 Wooster Street, 212-219-3531). It was there, while watching Rebecca and Stephanie debate whether 25/32 or 26/32 fit better, that I learned that the very dark blue that I had for years considered an unwearable relic of stiff 1950s denim had once again become the jeans color of choice. The girls enjoyed our stop at **Anna Sui** (113 Greene Street, 212-941-8406; www.annasui.com), too. We stopped at lots of other places, stores that would have been intimidating if I were shopping on my own. We priced dresses at the **Nicole Miller** boutique (134 Prince Street, 212-343-1362; www.nicolemiller.com), bath oils and fragrances at a shop along West Broadway, spent a few minutes admiring colorful, playful decorative objects and works of art at **Pop International Galleries** (473 West Broadway, 212-533-4262; www.popinternational.com). We somehow managed to miss the **Kate Spade** shop (454 Broome Street, 212-274-1991; www.katespade.com), but I suspect on our next trip that will be a prime destination. Then we had lunch at **Tennessee Mountain** (143 Wooster Street, 212-431-3993), which has the great advantage of being in the heart of SoHo but feeling reassuringly like any barbecue/big salad/hamburger restaurant anywhere, despite the geographic implication of its name. We even let Stephanie and Rebecca leave the restaurant a few minutes ahead of us and walk up Wooster Street alone, reveling in their temporary independence. Everything about that day was really fun and not nearly as expensive as it could have been. The same general itinerary, with allowances made for openings and closings as months pass, should work for any mother-daughter team; it's really a day of shopping as recreation, with the added benefit of walking in a vibrant landmark neighborhood along streets lined with architecturally unique buildings.

The pleasures of SoHo aren't limited to high-schoolers and their mothers, of course. It's a wonderful place for adults to walk, singly or together. If you don't want to shop, visit the galleries. If you want to avoid being stuck indoors on a lovely day, admire the cast-iron facades and occasional dramatic masonry buildings. My husband and I especially enjoyed a SoHo trip on a mild, slightly snowy day at the end of December several years ago. We took the train to the city specifically to see a gallery exhibit of Berenice Abbott's photographs of New York. In keeping with the unadventurous spirit of the day, we had lunch at Tennessee Mountain and glanced into the windows of a few more galleries. We lingered longer than I thought necessary at **Smith & Hawken** (394 West Broadway, 212-925-1190; www.smithandhawken.com), whose stores, like its catalogs, are filled with gardening tools and related items that are both useful and attractive. My husband still uses an elegant trowel-and-digging-fork set from Smith and Hawken that one of our neighbors gave him more than a decade ago. It's difficult to imagine that most people living near the Smith & Hawken shop in SoHo have much need of such utensils unless they have a roof garden, patio, or sturdy balcony, but some of the store's offerings could well appeal to indoor as well as outdoor gardeners. The store is housed in a cast-iron building that is part of SoHo's unique architectural identity.

Art, accessories, and architectural facades aside, it's possible to focus almost entirely on food and kitchen life on a walk around SoHo. You can buy delicacies to take home, or just browse among the produce, baked goods, and utensils. **Dean & DeLuca** (560 Broadway, 212-431-1691; www.deandeluca.com) was in its original long, narrow Prince Street quarters when I first ventured into its tempting but pricey premises in 1983. It has since moved to Broadway. Dean and DeLuca is a bustling place; its interior is filled with people browsing and buying. The crowded sidewalks just outside make Broadway seem less like the edge of SoHo than like an outpost of midtown Manhattan, but once inside the store, the world becomes quite rarefied again. The candy counter sells amazingly elaborate chocolates; some pieces cost more than a large supermarket candy bar, but they are also more beautiful. Particularly intriguing was what looked like a miniature caramel apple for $7. It turned out to be an apple-shaped truffle made of dark and white chocolate, filled with caramel-apple ganache, dipped in milk chocolate, coated with chopped hazelnuts, and mounted on a stick—very convincing and very elegant. The loosely wrapped chunks of Poilâne bread, flown in from the legendary Parisian bakery, also caught my eye, though I resisted the temptation to buy some, reminding myself that good bread has become widely available throughout the suburbs.

Gourmet Garage (453 Broome Street, 212-941-5850; www.gourmetgarage.com; additional Manhattan locations) is a quirky sort of place, almost a supermarket, but not a place you go for paper towels. Gourmet Garage was founded in 1981, originally serving as a wholesale distribution company of then-hard-to-find items such as radicchio; its SoHo warehouse opened in 1992. It's bright and spacious, a purveyor of interesting produce and dairy products, among other things, in a self-service, relatively unpretentious setting.

For a wonderful array of cookware, bakeware, and other useful kitchen stuff in a range of prices and brands, **Broadway Panhandler** (477 Broome Street at Wooster, 212-966-3434) is my favorite. Housed in more than 7,000 square feet of high-ceilinged, Corinthian-columned space, it provides ambience as well as everything you need to stock your kitchen. My colorful array of plastic cutting boards, selected at my daughter's urging during a recent trip to the city, brightens my dish drainer to such an extent that I'm sorry I didn't give in to Rebecca's enthusiasm and get more than three. She would have been happy to bring home a much wider variety of purchases from the store's thousands of offerings, which range from highly portable kitchen tools to somewhat portable cookbooks and bakeware to impossible-to-take-back-on-the-train items from Cuisinart, Krups, and Kitchen-Aid. Broadway Panhandler is open seven days a week and hosts various special events, such as cookbook signings and cookery demonstrations, so a visit there may turn into an educational trip as well as a shopping adventure.

There's a lot of mainstream shopping in SoHo, too. On West Broadway and surrounding streets you'll also come across such familiar (and variably affordable) shops as Gap, Rockport, Coach, and Prada, but their presence doesn't overwhelm the one-of-a-kind shops. The **Museum of Modern Art Design Store** (81 Spring Street, 646-613-1367; www.momastore.org), which opened in 2001, fits right in to the neighborhood's arts-oriented ambience, with its offerings of furniture, lighting, books, toys, household accessories and other items inspired by MoMA's collections. There is also an outpost of the Guggenheim Museum in the area—not just a store, but a branch museum. The **Guggenheim Museum SoHo** (575 Broadway, 212-423-3500, www.guggenheim.org) is open Thursday through Monday from 11 AM to 6 PM and, of course, it has a museum shop.

There's a stretch of Mercer Street between Spring and Broome Streets that focuses on shops designed to appeal to affluent parents who love to buy their children whimsical toys and fanciful clothes that you won't find at the local Baby Gap or Toys "R" Us. **Chimera** (77 Mercer Street, 212-334-4730) sells a tempting assortment of toys and sundries, and the clothes and other items on display at **Just for Tykes** (83 Mercer Street, 212-274-

9121) are lavish. **The Enchanted Forest** (85 Mercer Street, 212-925-6677) especially caught my eye, perhaps because of its delightful fairy-tale name; it sells books and toys, including a wonderful array of stuffed animals. The stores were empty of customers when I was there on a sunny weekday in December three months after the terrorist attack on the World Trade Center. Even for a weekday, it was too empty. I hope by the time you read this that the comfortable balance between frantically crowded and distressingly quiet will have returned.

SoHo is filled with places to eat, either as part of a day's exploring or as destinations in their own right. Two survivors from my commuting days are the **Broome Street Bar** (363 West Broadway, 212-925-2086), where my office mates and I went for hamburgers, and the **Cupping Room Café** (359 West Broadway, 212-925-2898), a high-ceilinged space made cozy by its exposed brick walls. The Cupping Room's Classic Cuban sandwich is piled with more than enough ham, pork, salami, and sausage to feed two carnivores for lunch, and its Iced Mocha is wonderful even in December. **Once Upon a Tart** (125 Sullivan Street, 212-387-8869) is a cozy place on a cozy street; as the name suggests, its baked goods are a main attraction. The **Country Café** (69 Thompson Street, 212-966-5417), a relative newcomer, serves unpretentious French food with a Moroccan flair and is a good choice for lunch or dinner. There are fancy places, famous places, and more expensive places scattered throughout the neighborhood; it's fun to read menus, check reviews, and hear what your friends have to say about a particular establishment, then enjoy a meal to suit mood and wallet.

Getting to SoHo is best done by public transportation. I still enjoy the walk east from the Christopher Street PATH station, but most people find it more of a trek than necessary, and if you plan to walk once you get to SoHo, it makes more sense to get closer to your destination. The Prince Street station on the N and R lines is a very convenient portal, and the C and E trains take you to the Spring Street station at the southwestern corner of the neighborhood. The Broadway-Lafayette stop of the F train is just east of SoHo proper; the 6 train (the Lexington Avenue local) stops at the Spring Street station on Lafayette Street, also a short walk east of SoHo.

Even if you have no desire to shop or even window shop, SoHo is worth a walk and a visit. It's a Historic District, so designated by the New York City Landmark Commission in 1973: cast-iron buildings, elaborately columned and corniced and often distinguished by large windows and distinctive pediments at the top, line block after block. To fully appreciate the details, it's often best to stand across the street and view the upper stories of the buildings at an angle. The **Haughwought Building** (488 Broadway at Broome Street) is generally considered the city's oldest surviving cast-iron building. Even if it weren't distinguished by its age—it dates to the late 1850s—it's an elegant structure in the style of a Venetian palazzo. Other especially noticeable and noteworthy buildings include several on Greene Street. The restful, cream-painted facade of **95 Greene Street** is one of my favorites; much of Greene Street, particularly the blocks between Canal and Grand Streets and Broome to Spring Streets, is lined with great cast-iron facades. *NOTE:* A building that looks its best at one moment may be sheathed in renovation netting or construction scaffolding a month or a year later, and buildings that were obscured by scaffolding last time I saw them may be stars when you walk past them.

4

Greenwich Village: Living Legend

Throughout the early 1960s, high-school students from the metropolitan area would hop aboard city-bound trains on Saturday mornings and disembark at Grand Central and the old, dignified Penn Station. From there, they spread out over Manhattan, to the 34th Street department stores, to the Donnell Library to research term papers, to the museums for a touch of culture, and to Greenwich Village to buy folk-music songbooks or venture into **Washington Square Park** and listen to people playing guitars and singing. In the 1970s, Washington Square became a place to avoid, with a reputation for drug-dealing and a general air of neglect, despite the bustle that continued to thrive around it, thanks to a constant stream of New York University students, local residents, and visitors. Over the decades, the park regained some of its old charm, though it still has a slightly scruffy air. The 1830s Greek Revival brick row houses on Washington Square North are as anachronistically charming as ever. Washington Memorial Arch still stands, abrupt yet perfectly in place, at the foot of Fifth Avenue, marking the start of the park; the marble arch, put up in 1892, replaced a wooden arch that had been designed to commemorate the centennial of George Washington's first presidential inauguration. NYU's reputation and selectivity are at all-time highs. All in all, the park presents a positive face. I don't know if I'd be happy about my own high-schooler spending Saturdays there on her own, but it is no longer a place to avoid.

The mere name of this neighborhood can conjure up an assortment of visions, depending upon your age and interests: artisans and shopkeepers in newly built row houses in the 1840s, wealthy New Yorkers in Washington Square townhouses in the 1890s, artists and poets in lofts and studios in the 1920s, or folksingers and politically active students in the 1960s. There's some truth in each of the images. Greenwich Village lends itself to exploration; almost every corner is worth turning, almost every block worth walking.

The richly varied area extends from 14th Street down to Houston Street, from the Hudson River to Broadway. Much of it is designated as the Greenwich Village Historic District. Washington Square Park, the neighborhood's major green space, is bounded by University Place on the east, MacDougal Street on the west, Waverly Place on the north, and West Fourth Street on the south; as these streets approach the park, they briefly become Washington Square East, West, North, and South respectively. The park occupies a former swamp that was drained in the late eighteenth century and used for such unglamorous purposes as public hangings and paupers' burials. Greenwich Village encompasses commercial Sixth Avenue, half-commercial, half-elegant Fifth Avenue, side streets filled with all sorts of residences, from classic brick and brownstone row houses and handsome stone churches to 1960s white-brick apartment buildings. It still has the occasional walkup apartment buildings; when my husband lived in a beautifully maintained old-fashioned walkup on Downing Street in the early 1970s, he paid $60 a month for a one-bedroom apartment. The building is still there, looking better than ever. The rent is probably twenty times higher now. In the absence of such personal landmarks as your own former fire escape, there are intriguing architectural anomalies to gaze at, such as Edna St. Vincent Millay's super-narrow house at **75½ Bedford Street** (shades of the Hogwarts Express, leaving from Platform 9¾), or the peaked-double-roof fairy-tale structure at **102 Bedford Street**. Mostly, the Village is a place to walk, not so much for a single specific sight as for mood and variety.

You can wander the intricate pattern of streets, immersing yourself in city sights for a morning, afternoon, or early evening. East of Sixth Avenue the streets run more or less at right angles to each other; west of Sixth Avenue, angles abound. That's because the irregular network of streets in the country settlement that was Greenwich Village in the early nineteenth century has been partly overlaid with standard New York rectangles. The result is a network of short blocks, streets that turn instead of running straight to the next intersection, and an overall sense of being in a place that was built without a master plan.

Your trip can be a modest one, aimless in a pleasant way, with the main goal just appreciating the variety and activity of city streets and glimpses of another way of life. Or it can be a pilgrimage to literary landmarks, places with political significance, or pretty streets. You can shop for food, clothes, antiques, and more. Sometimes my husband and I drive into the city on a weekend morning, find a parking space (easier on summer weekends than at other times of year), walk, peek into store windows, and have lunch. Or you can make the trip in late afternoon, see a movie after walking, then have dinner and go home, not having spent more money than you would have at home but feeling as though you've done something a bit more exciting than dinner and a movie in the suburbs. **John's Pizzeria** (278 Bleecker Street, between Sixth and Seventh Avenues, 212-243-1680) is fun if you have time to wait your turn at this very popular and traditional spot. The pizza is good, with thin, crisp crust and flavorful sauce; the surroundings are vibrant—and when you're done with dinner you're in the midst of the unthreatening bustle of Bleecker Street.

The irregular polygon that includes **Grove Street, Barrow Street, Commerce Street, and Morton Street** and is bordered on the west by Hudson Street, is full of brick row houses, reminders that Greenwich Village was, indeed, a village once. You can get lost in your wanderings in this part of the Village, since the streets meet at varying angles and run in no particular sequence, but that is part of the appeal. The beautiful brick complex centered on the church of **St. Luke's-in-the-Fields** (485 Hudson Street, between Barrow and Christopher Streets) evokes another time and place as well. St. Luke's was built as a chapel for Trinity Church in the early 1820s and was largely destroyed by fire in 1981; it has been partly restored. I like to peek into the private gardens of **Grove Court,** visible through the gate on Grove Street just east of Hudson Street. This is a direct route from the Christopher Street PATH station to the more commercial parts of the Village, but it still manages to feel tucked away in another century. Nearby is **17 Grove Street,** built in the 1820s and one of the few surviving wooden homes in Manhattan. There are houses with shutters, window boxes, and small dormers everywhere you look; larger structures, like **39** and **41 Commerce Street,** a pair of imposing brick homes with mansard roofs, add a slightly more pronounced touch of romance to the surroundings. Aaron Burr, once vice president of the United States and probably the most famous American ever to be disgraced in a duel (he killed Alexander Hamilton in 1802), lived on the site of **17 Commerce Street,** and Washington Irving is said to have written *The Legend of Sleepy Hollow* at **11 Commerce Street.** On Sundays I've often been tempted to linger in this picture-book charming neighborhood and gazed longingly several times at the menu at **Grange Hall** (50 Commerce Street at Barrow Street, 212-924-5246), knowing it's a good place for brunch; it's always been crowded, though, and we've never gone beyond the front door. In fact, it's open seven days a week and serves lunch and dinner, so a weekday afternoon trip would probably yield a shorter wait and a chance to enjoy a good soup, sandwich, and salad. Or better still, call ahead and make a reservation. A block or so away, **Petite Abeille** (466 Hudson Street at Barrow Street, 212-741-6479), the first in a small chain of Belgian restaurants, has several tables outside in good weather to supplement the seating inside the small restaurant. They are great places to enjoy the street scene as well as to indulge in waffles and other treats.

Throughout the neighborhood, there are other enclaves where blocks of historic residential buildings are interspersed with neighborhood shops. The street plans lend themselves to controlled wandering—that is, you can get a little lost but not irrevocably so, since you will almost certainly end up at either Hudson Street (which becomes Eighth Avenue above 14th Street), Seventh Avenue, or Sixth Avenue. Although all three major north-south thoroughfares do make a slight angle as they head south toward narrow lower Manhattan, they don't do anything completely unpredictable. One appealing streetscape of small, mostly brick houses includes **Bank, Perry, Charles,** and **West 11th Streets** east of and south of where Bleecker Street and Hudson Street come to a point at Abingdon Square. Across Hudson Street, along Greenwich Street and west of it, **Bethune** and neighboring streets offer more glimpses of a cozy neighborhood within a neighborhood. Among the most appealing are the row of houses dating to 1837 at 19–29 Bethune, and the two houses from the same year at 128 and 130 Bank Street, both west of Greenwich Street. Even the D'Agostino's supermarket at the corner of Greenwich and Bethune Streets is pretty, discreetly occupying a mellow-toned brick building. Nearby, **Nadine's** (99 Bank

Street at Greenwich Street, 212-924-3165) has big windows that offer great views both into the restaurant and out to the streets. At the corner of Bleecker and West 11th Streets, the **Magnolia Bakery** (401 Bleecker Street, 212-462-2572) offers very pretty cupcakes topped with swirled pastel-toned icing, as well as a variety of other treats, such as miniature cheesecakes and full-size German chocolate cake, to name just a few. For a non-food treat, window shop at **Les Pierre Antiques** (369 Bleecker Street, 212-243-7740). For something to read while you enjoy your Magnolia cupcakes, or just to browse, head for **Partners & Crime** (44 Greenwich Avenue, 212-243-0440) for mysteries, or the **Biography Bookshop** (400 Bleecker Street at 11th Street, 212-807-8655), which specializes in biographies but carries other subjects as well. In fact, it's nearly impossible to avoid book shops in the Village.

Hudson Street itself is full of restaurants, bakeries, takeout food stores, and other shops. It's also home to the **White Horse Tavern** (567 Hudson Street at West 11th Street, 212-243-9260), a bar with a long and illustrious past, best known for having been popular with generations of writers and artists, including Dylan Thomas. The **view down Hudson Street from Abingdon Square** presents a delightful, old-fashioned urban image of low-rise buildings, varied storefronts, trees, and people walking and shopping.

Walking along that stretch of Hudson Street, you'll be tempted to stop for a snack or other treat at almost every shop front. The **Cowgirl Hall of Fame** (519 Hudson Street at West 10th Street, 212-633-1133) has outdoor tables to relax at in good weather, a window full of friendly, colorful odds and ends, and a menu emphasizing Southern and Southwestern food. A few more steps will take you to **Ready to Eat** (525 Hudson Street, 212-2291013), which specializes in takeout meals, including home-cooked entrées, side dishes, salads and other foods; it's open daily from 11 AM to 10 PM. **Elixir Juice Bar** (523 Hudson Street, 212-352-9952, with its almost surgical array of juicing equipment, should be able to satisfy any thirst. All those temptations, and you haven't even walked a full block yet.

For a walk in a more formal setting, the blocks of **West 10th** and **West 11th Streets** (and to some extent West 9th and West 12th Streets) between Fifth and Sixth Avenues are long and beautiful, though they run in the familiar Manhattan grid pattern, which takes away a little of the romance. Mid-nineteenth-century rows like 20–38 West 10th Street set the tone, and even the occasional newer, taller apartment buildings don't seriously disrupt it. There are two beautiful churches to admire, as well. The Episcopal **Church of the Ascension** (36-38 Fifth Avenue at 10th Street), a Gothic Revival brownstone structure, was designed by Richard Upjohn in 1840 and remodeled in the 1880s by Stanford White, of McKim, Mead & White. It has stained-glass windows by John LaFarge (you can see other LaFarge stained glass in the American Wing at the Metropolitan Museum of Art); Augustus Saint-Gaudens did the marble altar sculpture. In short, the church constitutes a mini–art-history lesson, as well as being a beautiful presence for all those who visit or worship there. The nearby **First Presbyterian Church** (48 Fifth Avenue between 11th and 12th Streets) was designed by Joseph Wells and built in 1846; the south transept, by McKim, Mead & White, was added in 1893.

A block away, the **Jefferson Market Library** (425 Sixth Avenue at 10th Street), once the Jefferson Market Courthouse and now a branch of the New York Public Library, stands in ornate solitude on a triangular block on the west side of Sixth Avenue. It was built in 1877 and designed by the firm of Vaux & Withers. Its tall tower, complete with a clock, is its most noticeable feature, but its striped exterior of red brick and gray granite is also distinctive. The building, vacant from 1945 to the mid-1960s, was threatened with demolition, but a neighborhood preservation group mobilized to save and restore it, and it became a branch library in 1967.

The name Jefferson Market dates to the first half of the nineteenth century. The market sheds built in 1833 were replaced by a masonry market building in 1883, which was in turn torn down in 1927, long after the courthouse was completed. Until the mid-1970s, there was also a jail on the site. The first was built in 1877 along with the courthouse; like the market building, it was torn down in 1927. The Women's House of Detention replaced them. This tall, forbidding structure, built in 1931, was a striking visual and social contrast to the library. I remember walking near it when I lived more or less in the neighborhood, on 13th Street at University Place, in the early 1970s. Many people recall hearing women calling out the narrow windows to friends and family in the streets below, though it never happened when I passed by. The Women's House of Detention was demolished in 1974. There is now a neighborhood garden on the site.

On the northeast corner of Ninth Street and Sixth Avenue, directly above the Ninth Avenue PATH station, a recently closed food shop called **Balducci's** used to tempt hungry residents and commuters with a vast array of delectables. Happily, not far away, a store with an even longer tradition survives. **C. O. Bigelow Apothecaries** (414 Sixth Avenue, 212-473-7324; www.bigelowchemists.com), a pharmacy whose history extends well back into the nineteenth century, is another intriguing retail spot. It fills prescriptions like any other neighborhood pharmacy, but it is also a popular shopping destination for those in search of interesting makeup and other beauty products, costume jewelry, and additional sundries.

For a more active, down-to-earth experience, venture a few blocks south on Sixth Avenue and watch the seemingly endless basketball game being played on the outdoor court at the corner of 3rd Street. Players leave over the years, but the excitement doesn't. The players are really good, and some people make a trip to the corner specifically to watch them play.

For food, take an afternoon stroll any day of the week along Bleecker Street, from west to east. You can buy several types of Italian bread at **Zito's** (259 Bleecker Street, 212-929-6139), Italian pastries at **Rocco's** (243 Bleecker Street, 212-242-6031) or **Bleecker Street Pastry** (245 Bleecker Street, 212-242-4959), sausages and other pork treats at **Faicco's Pork Store** (260 Bleecker Street, 212-243-1974). Or, crossing Sixth Avenue, you might stop at a coffeehouse for rest and renewal. Several classic ones, **Caffe Reggio** (119 MacDougal Street, 212-475-9557), **Caffe Borgia** (185 Bleecker Street at MacDougal Street, 212-674-9589), and **Caffe Dante** (81 MacDougal Street south of Bleecker Street, 212-982-5275), provide both refreshment and atmosphere, as they have for years. Caffe Reggio, opened in 1927, is the oldest of the three.

Bleecker Street changes from block to block, from the fringes of the elegantly cozy row house neighborhoods to the west to the walkup apartments near Sixth Avenue to the coffeehouse/restaurant/nightclub mood farther east. The famous Berenice Abbott photograph of Zito's in the 1930s shows a front window that looks very much like the one that's there now; entering the bakery is like stepping into history, except that the bread is fresh and delicious. This is by no means the only great food street in the Village, but it is an especially tempting one. The more you walk and explore, the more you will find, and the hungrier you will become.

If you choose to plan your trip around theater or other organized entertainment, the possibilities are almost endless: a trip to the Minetta Lane Theater (see chapter 14) or an evening at legendary folk/blues/rock entertainment spots like the **Bottom Line** (15 West 4th Street at Mercer Street, 212-997-4144) or the **Bitter End** (147 Bleecker Street, between Thompson Street and LaGuardia Place, 212-673-7030). Newspapers or magazines such as *New York* magazine or *Time Out New York* will list enough venues and attractions for many trips.

Several half-hidden places are worth a visit during a trip to the village. **Washington Mews,** which runs from University Place to Fifth Avenue just north of Washington Square, is not so much hidden as discreetly inaccessible; though you can see it well enough and can even walk through it, it is closed to most vehicular traffic. Its north side consists of nineteenth-century stables that were remodeled in 1916; the south side of the mews contains twentieth-century buildings constructed to maintain the mood of the earlier ones. **MacDougal Alley,** off MacDougal Street just north of Washington Square Park, has much the same feeling. **Milligan Place,** dating to 1852, is off the west side of Sixth Avenue between 10th and 11th Streets. **Patchin Place,** a few years its senior, is off 10th Street between Sixth and Greenwich Avenues. Both are peaceful-looking cul-de-sacs lined with walkup apartment buildings; their locations off busy streets is part of their charm. Patchin Place was known as a writers' enclave in the 1920s; residents included poet e. e. cummings, journalist John Reed, and novelist Theodore Dreiser.

If you want to explore yet another block or two of picture-book city streets, head south of NYU and east of Sixth Avenue. Slightly less formal than the Fifth Avenue–Sixth Avenue rectangle of 9th, 10th, 11th, and 12th Streets and tucked away south of Washington Square Park, the quiet residential blocks of MacDougal and Sullivan Streets between Bleecker and West Houston Streets reflect a 1920s renovation of mid-nineteenth-century housing. The result, now designated the **MacDougal-Sullivan Gardens Historic District,** serves as a relaxing closing punctuation mark to a neighborhood that changes mood sharply when you cross Houston Street and enter the bustling commercial grasp of SoHo. That will give you a good opportunity to stop by the one-of-a-kind **Peanut Butter & Co.** (240 Sullivan Street, between Bleecker and West 3rd Streets, 212-677-3995) to sample delicious variations on peanut-butter sandwiches and get a taste of other peanut-butter creations.

Finding Your Way

The Village is a challenging place to drive or park, but an easy one to reach by public transportation. The Christopher Street and 9th Street PATH stations take you to various hearts of the Village if you are coming from New Jersey. A variety of subway trains will take you from Grand Central Terminal, Penn Station, or points within the city to at least one of the Village's several subway stations, and you can pick up a subway map at token booths. Take the A, C, E, F, or V to West 4th Street, or take the 1, 2, or 9 to Christopher Street/Sheridan Square. Several bus routes, such as the M20 (which goes down Seventh Avenue and up Hudson Street and Eighth Avenue) and the M2, M3, and M5 (which all go down Fifth Avenue but return uptown via several northbound avenues), will work, too, if you have the time and patience. Keep in mind that Greenwich Village covers a lot of territory, so check street and subway maps to pinpoint your destination.

5

Chelsea: Croissants and History

■ ■ ■ ■ ■ ■ ■ ■ ■

Chelsea conjures up many images, including a few unexpected ones. It's the site of the family farm of Clement Clarke Moore, who is considered the author of the wryly idyllic poem "A Visit from St. Nicholas," more widely known as "'Twas the Night Before Christmas." It's the low-rise neighborhood whose tree-lined streets are still graced by brick townhouses and the nostalgically private General Theological Seminary. It's the waterfront neighborhood that gets great sunlight, unobscured by the newly developed Chelsea Piers complex. It's the gritty industrial strip still laced with an unused elevated rail line and anchored on its southern end by a huge factory building, once the Nabisco plant, now home to the trendy media companies and fashionable food shops of Chelsea Market. It's the blocks between Tenth and Eleventh Avenues where warehouses and factories are being transformed into art galleries. What SoHo was once, Chelsea may be now.

Technically, Chelsea starts at 14th Street and runs north well into the 20s, but from an architectural standpoint its borders are a bit looser. As you head north, soon after Hudson Street turns into Eighth Avenue and the street grid straightens out after its last rebellious angle at Abingdon Square, you reach 14th Street and begin to sense you aren't in the Village anymore. There are buildings with "Chelsea" in their names as far east as Sixth Avenue, but they seem more appropriate from Eighth Avenue west to the river. The transition from the Flatiron District on the east and Greenwich Village to the south is not abrupt. As you exit the PATH station at Sixth Avenue and 14th Street and head west on 15th Street, it would be hard to say just what the neighborhood was called, for example, but the block is very pleasant, lined with row houses and bustling with construction and renovation. Cross a few streets and the look changes. Fifteenth Street west of Seventh Avenue is even nicer, with an especially attractive row of brick houses on the south side of the street. St. Vincent's Hospital adds a touch of institutional solidity to the area and keeps the streetscape busy. As you walk west on 15th Street past St. Vincent's and approach the busy corner of Ninth Avenue, you may notice a lovely little building bridge daintily spanning 15th Street west of Ninth Avenue, crossing from one massive building to another.

A relaxing way to start an excursion in Chelsea—and one that doesn't resemble anything you'll find in even the most *au courant* suburb—is to stop at **Chelsea Market** (75 Ninth Avenue, between 15th and 16th Streets, 212-247-1423), located in an enormous old industrial building. Chelsea Market is a good place to have lunch, though if you plan to do any serious shopping you might want to save this for last so you won't have to carry bags full of oddly shaped, fragrant, or perishable bundles through the streets as you explore and visit art galleries.

The market is surprisingly easy to miss, despite the huge size of the building. The signs outside are not flashy, and the look is not obviously glamorous. This is a place that combines wholesale and retail commerce with office space. The Chelsea Market building is a production facility for some businesses, so when you walk through, trying to decide what to buy for lunch or snack, you see people working in unadorned kitchens, creating fashionable food. There is a plant shop near the entrance and a basket shop at the far end of the corridor, but it's the food that catches the mind and eye. Among the attractions are Hale and Hearty Soups, the Manhattan Fruit Exchange (akin to an indoor farm stand, complete with decorative displays of pumpkins in October), and Ronnybrook Farm Dairy. The second store you will see as you enter from Ninth Avenue is **Eleni's Cookies** (212-255-7990; www.elenis.com), purveyors of beautifully decorated cookies at prices (generally starting at $3 each) that make you feel you ought to admire them for a day or two before eating them. Eleni's sells muffins, cupcakes, and gift packages of cookies.

Two of my favorite spots at Chelsea Market are Amy's Bread and Fat Witch Bakery. **Fat Witch** (212-807-1335 or 888-41witch/419-4824; www.fatwitch.com), next door to Eleni's (presenting an almost diabolical combination of temptations), specializes in brownies. When I stopped by on the day before Halloween, it was featuring pumpkin brownies, in addition to its usual array of creatively named brownies: the classic, intensely chocolatey Fat Witch; the Blonde Witch, essentially a soft, rectangular chocolate-chip cookie only better; the Breakfast Witch, with oatmeal as well as walnuts and coffee in it, making it a socially acceptable way to start your day; and the Red Witch, with dried cherries. **Amy's Bread** (at Chelsea Market, 212-462-4323; also in Hell's Kitchen at 672 Ninth Avenue, between 46th and 47th Streets, 212-977-977-2282; and on the Upper East Side, 972 Lexington Avenue, between 70th and 71st Streets, 212-537-0270; www.amysbread.com) offers a more varied set of temptations. The bread is wonderful. So are the smaller items, such as twists and rolls. There's a great range of specialties, including especially good black olive bread and semolina bread with golden raisins and fennel, as well as less-adorned treats such as rustic Italian and whole wheat breads. Conveniently, Amy's Bread at Chelsea Market doubles as a small, informal restaurant, where you can order a sandwich and beverage at the bread counter and then enjoy them while reading a section of the day's paper. At least, that's what I did, with a delicious vegetarian hummus sandwich and peppermint tea.

When you leave Chelsea Market and turn north on Ninth Avenue, the world becomes more functional and less picturesque for a few blocks. Nondescript housing projects line the west side of the avenue for several blocks, but as you look east you'll notice small-scale buildings and tree-shaded sidewalks. And then you get to 20th Street. Two things make this worth noting. The first landmark is **La Bergamote** (169 Ninth Avenue, southwest corner of 20th Street, 212-627-9010). This corner bakery-café has an enticing menu posted in its window, with names and prices of dozens of mostly French pastries and confections: peach charlotte, $4; chocolate mice (the size of real mice), $3.25; sandwiches, $5. The menu is nice, but the display inside is even better. Everything is perfectly detailed, fruit tarts glistening, chocolate coatings smooth and dark, shapes precise. They taste almost as good as they look; my family and I shared carefully divided pieces of a chocolate mouse and a tiny chocolate-hazelnut cake, and we would have been happy to pounce on each other's uneaten portions, but there weren't any. With the mood set by the magic of a Paris patisserie transported to Manhattan—the women behind the counter spoke English to customers and French to each other—I turned west onto 20th Street, having forgotten that it's the block anchored by the General Theological Seminary. As I walked past the beautiful Greek Revival brick row houses on the south side of the street I realized that the buildings were even nicer than others I had been admiring that day. A plaque identified several of the houses (406–418 West 20th Street) as Cushman Row; details such as the iron fence and brownstone-framed doorways are part of the charm, but it's the overall effect of this row and its neighbors that makes the block so spectacular. On the north side of the street, the iron fence and locked gate of the grounds of the **General Theological Seminary** (175 Ninth Avenue, 212-243-5150) provide a parklike vista most unusual for New York, with tree-shaded lawns and a Gothic Revival quadrangle. The mini-neighborhood is known as Chelsea Square, and even the buildings outside the fence fronting on the north side of 20th Street near Ninth Avenue have a wonderful nineteenth-century quality, but it's the West Building, constructed in the 1830s, that is the centerpiece of the view when you stand in front of the 20th Street gate. The grounds are open to the public on weekday afternoons, but you have to enter through the twentieth-century building on Ninth Avenue; lovely as the setting is, peeking longingly though the 20th Street fence at the peace and privacy inside may be more than half the fun. The seminary, founded in 1817, is the oldest Episcopal Seminary in the United States. Clement Clarke Moore taught at the seminary from 1821 to 1850 and donated the land on which it now stands.

Zigzagging back and forth from Eighth to Tenth Avenues, you almost never lose the sense that this is an older, more charming New York. On Ninth Avenue just north of 21st Street there are even three little wooden buildings. One of my favorite streets is West 24th between Ninth and Tenth Avenues, where an unexpected row of beautiful small brick row houses on the north side of the street faces the massive presence of the London Terrace apartment complex. London Terrace, built in 1930, occupies the whole block between 23rd and 24th Streets. The low buildings on the north side of 24th Street are decades older and are set back in small yards, an unusual sight in the city. The contrast between the two kinds of residential development—small mid-nineteenth century and large but nicely detailed early twentieth century—makes the block an especially appealing part of a Chelsea walk.

Small-scale buildings and tree-shaded sidewalks give way to big buildings in an industrial—increasingly, postindustrial—landscape west of Tenth Avenue. The Tenth Avenue block is dramatic; it's where the new, fashionable galleries, many of them with names already well known in SoHo or on Madison Avenue, have installed themselves, with discreetly lettered doorways and unexpected plate glass amid the old brick facades. This is the block that the High Line passes through. Officially known as West Side Elevated Freight Railroad when it was built in 1934, the High Line has for years been under threat of demolition and is the subject of a spirited preservation battle led by an organization known as Friends of the High Line. Seen from the ground, it simply looks like an out-of-service elevated railway, not so different from the elevated lines that used to run above several Manhattan avenues. The difference is that this was a freight line that ran not between buildings but in some cases through them; the track bed now stops at sealed-up openings in some of the buildings the line once served. It runs from 34th Street to the Meat Packing District at 14th Street; a section south of that has already been demolished. The large factories and industrial buildings on this block once benefited from the extremely convenient rail transportation the High Line provided.

The Friends of the High Line would like to preserve the rail line and turn it into a public promenade with safe, legal access. The federal government's rails-to-trails program has helped preserve and transform thousands of miles of railroad rights-of-way elsewhere in the country, and it is hoped that the same program can be put into effect to preserve the viaduct for use as a recreational trail with great urban views.

Trains have not run along this line for years, and much of the industrial activity of the area has gone as well. It's only as you walk down each block that the evolution becomes clear; a building that looks from a distance like a deserted manufacturing facility turns out, as you approach the entrance, to be one of the area's many sleek galleries. Among the familiar names are **Sonnabend** (536 West 22nd Street, 212-627-1018) and **Paula Cooper** (534 West 21st Street, 212-255-1105, and 521 West 21st Street, 212-255-5247), both well-known SoHo pioneers now established in Chelsea. **Cheim & Read** (521 West 23rd Street, 212-242-7727) represents both painters and photographers. **Jim Kempner Fine Art** (501 West 23rd Street, 212-206-6872) occupies a strikingly designed building on the northwest corner of 23rd Street and Tenth Avenue and specializes in contemporary prints and works on paper. The galleries extend well up into the twenties, with a particular concentration on 24th Street.

Also in a renovated warehouse in the emerging gallery district is the **Dia Center for the Arts** (548 West 22nd Street, 212-989-5566; www.diacenter.org). For more than two decades this institution has supported a variety of artistic endeavors, with an emphasis on large and unconventional works. Its 40,000 square feet of exhibition space house a variety of exhibits by contemporary artists. It also sponsors literature and performing-arts programs, has an ongoing series of poetry readings, and offers a number of arts-education programs. The center is open Wednesday through Sunday.

Walking west toward Eleventh Avenue, you approach the Hudson River and the wonderful West Side light that can be so surprising if you are used to the shadowy streets of midtown Manhattan. On the far side of Eleventh Avenue is the equally surprising **Chelsea Piers Sports and Entertainment Complex** (between 17th and 23rd Streets, Piers 59–62 and the Hudson River, 212-336-6666; www.chelseapiers.com), the largest sports center in New York City. Some of the activities it offers are things you can do on almost any high-school field, or in your local science museum. All the same, even if you have the wide-open space of suburbia at your disposal, there's a certain glamour about coming to Chelsea Piers to skate. There are two all-season indoor ice-skating rinks and two outdoor seasonal roller-skating rinks. The Sky Rink offers youth and adult ice-hockey leagues, as well as private classes and recreational skating time; the Field House has batting cages, an open gym, rock climbing for adults and for children aged four and older, basketball and playing fields, even a toddler gym and a bowling alley. The year-round Golf Club is a multitiered outdoor range, with fifty-two heated hitting stalls and a 200-yard artificial-turf fairway. Chelsea Piers offers daily sports packages—the Gold Passport and the Silver Passport—that give you the opportunity to participate in several activities.

Chelsea offers an abundance of art and architecture, but the neighborhood is also a wonderful place to lunch, snack, dine, or just buy a few things to take home. There is hardly a block that doesn't offer at least one appealing restaurant or food shop. **Pepe Giallo** (253 Tenth Avenue at 25th

Street, 212-242-6055) is known for its delicious and very affordable sandwiches and pasta. Thanks to its bright-yellow facade, **Sandro's** (200 Ninth Avenue between 22nd and 23rd Streets, 212-633-8033) will catch your eye as you approach it. When I walked past, two women were sitting at a window table, enjoying what looked like a leisurely lunch and large glasses of red wine—apparently an ideal break in a day of gallery-hopping, window-shopping, or, perhaps, ordinary work. A block away, the **Empire Diner** (210 Tenth Avenue at 22nd Street, 212-243-2736) was bustling, as it often is. It's a classic-looking diner, and open all night, so it can be a feast for the eyes even if you aren't hungry. The **Krispy Kreme** doughnut shop (265 West 23rd Street, 212-620-0111) is a cheering sight for another reason: the doughnuts are wonderful. Although the West 23rd Street shop was the first Krispy Kreme in the city, my favorite used to be the large, clean, welcoming Krispy Kreme shop at 5 World Trade Center, which was destroyed in the terrorist attack of September 11, 2001. I was glad to find out from the Krispy Kreme Web site (www.krispykreme.com) that all the people who worked at the downtown Krispy Kreme survived.

6

The Flatiron District: A Familiar Name, But Have You Been There?

When I was growing up on East 22nd Street between Second and Third Avenues, the blocks west of Lexington Avenue were a mysterious zone, quiet on weekends, populated by very few people. There were some prewar apartment buildings, and industrial loft buildings, but the neighborhood lacked definition: it was neither Gramercy Park nor Murray Hill, neither Stuyvesant Town nor Stuyvesant Square. Those same half-forgotten, quiet blocks of the lower twenties and upper teens have come to life, or, more accurately, back to life. The Flatiron District, named for the triangular building that has long been a landmark at the corner of 23rd Street where Fifth Avenue and Broadway crisscross, bustles with shoppers, restaurant-goers, and office staffers in a way that was almost unimaginable a few decades ago. The area known as the Ladies' Mile when it was the hub of the fashionable retail trade in the late nineteenth and early twentieth centuries once again roars with traffic and hums with the conversations of shoppers. At the southern fringe of the neighborhood, the Greenmarket at Union Square has been thriving for years, bringing fresh farm produce and trendy tastes of country life to the city. So the borderlands of my childhood neighborhood, those blocks from 14th to 23rd Streets, within an avenue or two of Fifth Avenue, have found an identity again.

There isn't any one destination to draw you to this area; rather, it's the overall feeling of being in a big city, with big buildings from another time, stores from every era, a few historic sites, and a lot of places to find good food. One way to encapsulate the experience is to stand on the east side of Fifth Avenue between 22nd and 23rd Streets at the entrance to the **Flatiron Building** (175 Fifth Avenue). Standing in front of this distinctive limestone building, which is a designated landmark in its own right and has been immortalized in the photography of Edward Steichen and the painting of Childe Hassam, you can look up Fifth Avenue at another of the icons of New York City, the majestic art deco mass of the Empire State Building, looming in the near distance. The Flatiron Building itself is best admired from a slight distance to the northwest so you can see the narrow angle of its north corner; the interior isn't really a place for the general public to visit, since this is an everyday office building.

The **Ladies' Mile Historic District** extends from 18th Street up to 23rd Street on Sixth Avenue, from just south of 15th Street to 24th Street on Fifth Avenue, and from 17th to 21st Streets on Broadway. It was the heart of fashionable New York shopping in the last decades of the nineteenth century and the first decade or so of the twentieth. Each avenue has a slightly different appearance and mood even now, with Sixth Avenue being rather mass-market despite its magnificent buildings, Fifth Avenue maintaining a certain elegance, and Broadway having some of the most interesting buildings and the worst traffic.

If this architectural vista intrigues you, a walk over to Sixth Avenue, home of the nineteenth-century shopping giants, may be a logical next step. The impact of the buildings is greater if you are coming up from 14th Street along Sixth Avenue, which is lined in the mid-teens with low buildings that look as thought they belong in an Edward Hopper painting. The tree-lined side streets, especially 15th and 16th Streets, offer tantalizing glimpses of brownstones that are much more appealing than the nondescript bustle of Sixth Avenue. Don't give up on Sixth Avenue, though: starting at 18th Street, it is lined with massive structures that were once occupied by great retail names of the past such as Siegel-Cooper, Hugh O'Neill, Simpson-Crawford, and B. Altman; the buildings have come back to life as mass-market chain stores. As a resident of New Jersey, which has a number of spectacularly upscale malls and many midlevel ones, as well as no sales tax on clothing, I long ago got out of the habit of clothes-shopping in New York City. Now that there is no New York sales tax on clothing purchases under $110, shopping has become more inviting. So although I still don't think of New York when I want to browse national chain stores, it is possible to combine a mall-style shopping trip with a walk through a neighborhood that represents a long-ago style of urban life.

Perhaps the most notable building is the former Siegel-Cooper building on the east side of Sixth Avenue between 18th and 19th Streets. It takes up the entire north/south block and goes almost all the way east to Fifth Avenue as well. It is now home to Bed Bath & Beyond, T.J. Maxx, and Filene's Basement, and although there is a stripped-down public space in the center of the building, it is hard to get a sense of what the original interior must have been like when there was a circular marble terrace on the ground floor, highlighted by a brass and marble statue/fountain. The exterior entrance is very impressive, with columns, carvings, and an enormous archway; it's worth crossing Sixth Avenue to get a good view. That is also the best vantage point for admiring the central tower over the center of this six-story giant. The old B. Altman building is directly across the street from the Siegel-Cooper building, on the west side of Sixth Avenue. Much simpler in style but very elegant, it now houses Today's Man. The bright-blue awnings at the first- and second-story windows make the building easy to spot, even if they don't quite fit the classical simplicity of the cast-iron facade of the structure. The Hugh O'Neill building, on the west side of Sixth Avenue between 20th and 21st Streets, is also cast iron. In comparison to the Siegel-Cooper splendor, it looks a bit small and not quite tall enough, but it's appealing in its own right, with round corner towers and a rather dainty pediment with the name "Hugh O'Neill" still perfectly legible. The Third Spanish Portuguese Cemetery, used from 1829 to 1851, is tucked away on West 21st Street just off Sixth Avenue; it's an intriguing relic, but the gate to the cemetery is locked and you can't read the inscriptions from the sidewalk. Between 21st and 22nd Streets, also on the west side of the avenue, there's a large Barnes & Noble bookstore in the elaborate building once occupied by the Adams Dry Goods Store.

On your way from the Sixth Avenue portion of the neighborhood to slightly more peaceful Fifth Avenue, you might want to stop at the **City Bakery** (3 West 18th Street, 212-366-1414). It can be very crowded at lunchtime, and as a suburban visitor I sometimes find it a little intimidating because everyone else looks so fashionable, but the food is so good and the serving arrangements so convenient that it's well worth a stop. If you plan an early lunch you should find plenty of tables available. Small and smaller round tables line the walls on either side of the cash register/baked-goods island. (The City Bakery is known for its croissants, but there's a lot more to the bakery story than that.) A delicious variety of creative salads, sandwiches, and other foods is available farther back in the room. The prewrapped half-sandwiches are filling without being so large that you won't have room for the vegetables and salads, which are sold by weight. When I ate there one late summer day, the chunks of Kirby cucumbers from the nearby Union Square greenmarket were delicious with crumbled feta cheese and a tangy lemony dressing, and roasted zucchini sticks were extremely good too. As well as making a perfect lunch stop, the City Bakery is a great place for sit-down or take-home snacks. The pretzel croissants and crème brûlée tarts are among my favorites.

Eighteenth Street has several other appealing shops. One is **Paper Access** (23 West 18th Street, 212-463-7035, www.paperaccess.com), which sells a sophisticated selection of paper (for both wrapping and writing/printing), envelopes, and accessories in a glamorously urban setting. Across the street, **Books of Wonder** (16 West 18th Street, 212-989-3270, www.booksofwonder.net) is the city's largest and oldest independent children's bookstore, and it's the kind of place you want to browse through even if you don't have young children. It sells classic and contemporary books of all kinds for children and has an extensive selection of old and rare books.

When you reach Fifth Avenue, the view east on the south side of 18th Street offers an almost painterly perspective of nineteenth-century commercial buildings with fire escapes running up the front of most of them. Fifth Avenue has been malled almost as much as Sixth Avenue has, but it isn't as cluttered, and the stores are a little more upscale: Gap instead of Old Navy, for example. The flagship **Barnes & Noble** (105 Fifth Avenue, 212-807-0099) is at the corner of Eighteenth Street, as it has been since 1932. Before the proliferation of superstores and Web sites, this was the place to find books.

If you've admired enough buildings and done enough window-shopping, you may want to take a break and visit the **Theodore Roosevelt Birthplace** (28 East 20th Street, 212-260-1616). The house is a reconstruction rather than an original, but it is evocative and filled with fascinating memorabilia. It is a brownstone on a surprisingly quiet stretch of 20th Street just off busy Fifth Avenue. When Theodore Roosevelt was born, in 1858, the neighborhood was a fashionable residential district, but by the turn of the century it had become commercial and the family had long since moved to West 57th Street. The house on 20th Street was torn down and replaced by a commercial structure in 1916, which in turn was demolished and replaced by the current structure in 1923; that home was rebuilt specifically to serve as a memorial to Roosevelt, who served as president of the United States from 1901 to 1909. Museum galleries were built on an adjoining lot. The Theodore Roosevelt Association donated the site to the National Park Service in 1963. It's wonderfully restful and quiet. The uniformed park rangers are refreshingly historical-minded, informal, and urban in tone.

One of the best parts of the visit is the gallery on the main floor, with fascinating photographs of Roosevelt's family and scenes of his public and private life, as well as many artifacts and mementos. The photograph of Theodore Roosevelt and his brother watching Abraham Lincoln's funeral cortege from a window of the house is particularly memorable. There is also a slightly more spacious gallery upstairs, with books and other memorabilia. The re-created rooms of the house itself, which you visit on a guided tour, are worth seeing, but not quite as gripping as the galleries. Much of the furniture is original and belonged to the family. The Theodore Roosevelt Birthplace is open from 10 AM to 5 PM Wednesday through Thursday, with guided tours given on the hour; the last tour starts at 4 PM. There is also a well-stocked gift shop, with a good choice of books pertaining to Roosevelt's life and times and a nice selection of postcards and other small items. Admission was a very reasonable $2 when I visited in early September 2001, which seemed extremely economical. This is a good place for anyone with an interest in Theodore Roosevelt or American history to visit; although small children might not find it interesting, children from the middle elementary grades on up probably will, especially if they have already learned a little about Roosevelt in school. The house really brings both a historical figure and a historical period to life.

On the Outside Looking In

If you walk a block east on 20th Street from the Theodore Roosevelt birthplace, you will find yourself at Irving Place, facing the elegant iron fence that surrounds **Gramercy Park**. Gramercy Park is the only private park in the city and is surrounded by a combination of rowhouses and early apartment buildings. Even though you cannot get into Gramercy Park without a key—and you cannot get a key unless you live in the immediate area or are a guest at the Gramercy Park Hotel (2 Lexington Avenue, 212-475-4320)—it's pleasant to peek through the railing and admire the Londonesque landscape. Gramercy Park occupies the block between 20th and 21st Streets; Lexington Avenue ends north of the park and resumes course as Irving Place south of the park.

Several buildings around the park stand out. The **National Arts Club** (15 Gramercy Park South) owns a forty-room mansion that was once two separate houses built in 1845; they were remodeled decades later by Calvert Vaux (who, along with Frederick Olmsted, designed Central Park) and became the home of Samuel Tilden, a governor of New York and candidate for president in 1876. Tilden won the popular vote by about 250,000 but was defeated in the Electoral College by Rutherford B. Hayes. The National Arts Club has owned the house since the early 1900s. The house has a special place in my family's personal lore: soon after my mother began teaching third grade in New York City in the mid-1950s, she took her class to the Roosevelt house. On the way there she glanced at the plaque in front of the National Arts Club and told her children that it was the home of Samuel Tilden, who had been president of the United States. As she described it, she was interrupted by an indignant, distinguished-looking older woman passing by, who said loudly and reproachfully, "Madam, Samuel Tilden was never president of the United States." And my mother, who was almost never wrong, corrected herself; she told the story for years afterward whenever anyone in the family was convinced on slight evidence that he or she was right about something. The **Players Club** (16 Gramercy Park South) is next door. It too was built in 1845 as a private home; after being purchased by the actor Edwin Booth it was remodeled in 1885 by Stanford White to serve as a club for theater professionals. Down the street, the simple, almost rural-looking **Brotherhood Synagogue** (144 East 20th Street) was once the Friends Meeting House, built in 1859.

On the way to the Roosevelt house you will probably have noticed a beautiful gray building at the southwest corner of Broadway and 20th Street. This is the **old Lord & Taylor building**. On my summer visit to the neighborhood, the rounded corner balcony/tower of the five-story cast-iron Lord & Taylor building was brightened with pots of lovely pink flowers and looked, for a moment, like a corner of Paris. A sign advertised full-floor lofts for rent, so apparently this is no longer a public building but one to admire from the outside only. This is by no means the first Lord & Taylor building. The firm was established on Catherine Street in 1826 by Samuel Lord, who was joined twelve years later by George Washington Taylor. The business moved uptown to Grand Street in 1852 and the Broadway section of the Ladies' Mile in the 1870s. Lord & Taylor moved to Fifth Avenue and 38th Street in 1914.

If you want to explore a few more densely packed retail blocks, continue down Broadway, whether to admire buildings or window displays, or, perhaps, even do some real shopping.

Fishs Eddy (889 Broadway at 10th Street, 212-420-9020) occupies a wonderful brick building that is as interesting as the tremendous array of dishes, china, and glassware inside the store. Built in the 1880s, this ornate structure was once the home of the Gorham Manufacturing Company, a name still associated with silverware. **ABC Carpet & Home** (888 Broadway at 18th Street, 212-473-3000) is a multistory store filled with elegant furnishings and accessories. The ground floor is dazzling and pricey enough to send a thrifty shopper scurrying to IKEA, but even if your funds won't stretch to ABC purchases, it's fun to explore the store—all ten floors of it. In addition to being a super-fashionable purveyor of furniture, antiques, all sorts of decorative accessories (such as fringed velvety throw pillows in the high two-figure price range), textiles, and floor coverings (sold across the street at 881 Broadway), ABC also has two restaurants: Pipa, featuring tapas and Latino cuisine, and Chicama (35 East 18th Street, 212-505-2233). There is also a food hall selling cheese, bread, chocolates, and other delicacies. Across Broadway just south of 18th Street you'll find **Paragon Sporting Goods** (867 Broadway, 212-255-8036). It is much larger than it looks from the front entrance and has items you wouldn't at first associate with New York City, from tennis racquets to swim goggles, sneakers to camping gear.

The north/south blocks are very short here. If you have come as far downtown as Paragon and it is a Monday, Wednesday, Friday, or Saturday, it's worth walking one more block to experience the **Greenmarket at Union Square,** whose northern tip is at Seventeenth Street and Broadway. Greenmarkets are New York City's open-air farmers' markets, open only to growers from the metropolitan region. The one at Union Square operates year-round and, like the city's other greenmarkets, sells more than the customary produce. Other popular items include dairy products, baked goods, jam, honey, maple syrup, and organic meats. The number of booths varies by season, but there is always something to tempt buyers.

Public transportation is the best way to get to the Ladies' Mile/Flatiron District/Gramercy Park area, especially on weekdays; traffic can be heavy and slow. There are PATH stations on Sixth Avenue at 14th and 23rd Streets, subway stations on Sixth Avenue, Broadway, and Park Avenue South, and bus stops almost everywhere, so if you are coming from Hoboken, Penn Station, or Grand Central Terminal, it's very conveniently located. The Flatiron Building itself is only a fifteen- or twenty-minute walk from Penn Station, but there's no really scenic route, so you might want to save your energy and use your MetroCard. Once you are here, you can enjoy the walk in any direction throughout the neighborhood.

7

The Far East Side:
A Vague Name for a
Varied Place

There is a lot more to the Upper East Side than a view of Central Park, the unattainable treasures of Madison Avenue boutiques, and well-dressed women with champagne-blonde hair. In fact, once you get as far east as Lexington Avenue, the atmosphere becomes less rarified. The image shifts from the sleek mélange of expensive shops, restaurant, and bakeries to a cozier if less elegant ambience that one might have thought had vanished half a century ago. Yes, Bloomingdale's, with its massive flagship store occupying the block between Lexington and Third Avenues and 59th and 60th Streets, presents itself as a sophisticated fashion source. But my paternal grandmother, who lived on East 55th Street, also east of the line of elegance, shopped there regularly, and the basement level of the store, immediately adjacent to a subway station, still feels as down-to-earth as it literally is. Yes, east of Lexington Avenue there are tall buildings all the way from 57th Street up to the vast hospital land of the 90s and 100s. But many of them rise abruptly at a side-street corner and are a jarring presence on avenues still lined with three-or four-story buildings, endless small ethnic restaurants, fruit-and-vegetable markets, little specialty shops that don't look trendy enough to call boutiques, and a surprising number of grocery stores.

In short, the area offers an intriguing mix of old and new, impersonal and charming, rich and everyday. Certainly there are specific destinations, but in a way the attraction is greater than the sum of its parts. It's a place to walk and pause and simply take the time to enjoy whatever you like most about being in a city. If you're a New Jersey day tripper, as I am, you might want to take the E train from Penn Station to the stop at 53rd Street and Lexington Avenue. After exiting through the **Citicorp Center** plaza (or stopping briefly to browse the center's atrium mall), you find yourself immediately facing a bustling, at first nondescript stretch of the avenue. As you start walking uptown, it quickly becomes apparent that the scenery is not all clutter and coffee shops. First to break the mood is **St. Peter's Church at Citicorp Center,** at 54th Street and Lexington Avenue; its angled roof vaguely echoes the much taller angle of the Citicorp Center itself. The beautiful **Central Synagogue,** at the corner of 55th Street and Lexington Avenue, is the oldest synagogue in the city in continuous use. A sandstone structure trimmed with limestone, it reflects a distinctive Moorish Revival style, most notable in its two elaborate towers. Built in the 1870s and modeled after a synagogue in Budapest, it was designated a city landmark in 1966 and a National Historic Landmark in 1975.

The intangible charm of being in a classic cityscape surfaces again on 57th Street east of Second Avenue, when after several blocks of sterility the wide crosstown street suddenly starts to look like the impossibly romantic and idealized New York of 1930s movies. It is lined with tall pre–World War II luxury apartment buildings. After enjoying the vista east on 57th Street, you might want to turn north on First Avenue, where you will be pleasantly surprised by glimpses of the lovely old houses on 58th Street east of First Avenue. Running parallel to First Avenue and one block east of it is **Sutton Place.** Once a tenement district in the shadow of giant gas tanks and known as Avenue A, it was redeveloped after World War I into an elegant residential neighborhood of apartment buildings and town houses. It's a nice place to walk in good weather, even if you are not visiting anyone in the neighborhood. Sutton Place becomes York Avenue at 59th Street and passes under the Queensboro Bridge.

Although the nearby **Queensboro Bridge,** which opened to traffic in 1909 and links Manhattan with Queens, doesn't have the cachet and charm of the Brooklyn Bridge, it isn't bad-looking. In fact, its intricate towers are quite impressive from nearby Manhattan streets, and the bridge makes a dramatic backdrop for the streetscape of this part of the east side. What's more, it's the bridge Simon and Garfunkel sing about in their lilting "59th Street Bridge Song (Feelin' Groovy)," and when you look at the bridge on a bright, sparkling day, you can understand why.

Bridgemarket occupies the tiled, vaulted spaces at the base of the Manhattan side of the bridge. The space served as a farmers' market in the early decades of the twentieth century and now houses a Food Emporium supermarket, a Terence Conran shop, and Conran's Guastavino, a multilevel restaurant serving eclectic food. **Guastavino** (409 East 59th Street, 212-80-2455) is named for the Spanish architect Rafael Guastavino, who designed the Queensboro Bridge vaults and other vaulted interiors, including the one at Grand Central Terminal and the main hall at Ellis Island. **Conran's** shop (407 East 59th Street, 212-755-9079) sells kitchenware, tableware, furniture, and other home-related items. I used to love shopping at the first generation of American Conran's shops in the early 1980s. I bought all sorts of things at the Conran's stores at Astor Place in Manhattan and Riverside Square Mall in New Jersey, from bright-red plastic kitchen storage bins to wallpaper and matching curtain fabric for my son's room; we even bought his first non-baby furniture—shiny, warm-toned pine dresser, bedside table, and grade-school size desk—at Conran's. The bedside table is still in what we continue to call Matt's room, and the dresser, which must be more than fifteen years old, went with him to his first New York apartment when he graduated from college. So for practical and sentimental reasons, I was glad to see the new version of Conran's.

From Bridgemarket, it's little more than a two-block walk to the **Mount Vernon Hotel Museum and Garden** (421 East 61st Street, 212-838-6876). Like the rest of the eastern fringe, the museum and garden are a bit off the beaten track, if rapid transit is the track in question. It's not inaccessible, just several blocks east of the nearest subway line and several blocks north or south of any crosstown bus. The house and garden, once set amid rolling fields in the countryside north of a much smaller New York City, haven't moved, but they now seem strikingly out of place on their East Side block, which is almost literally in the shadow of the Queensboro Bridge. The anachronism is part of the charm, of course, and the link to the past is quite real. Whether it is worth a stop or a visit depends on how interested you are in small pieces of history.

Formerly known as the Abigail Adams Smith Museum, the Mount

Vernon Hotel Museum and Garden is owned and maintained by the Colonial Dames of America. It occupies a gracious and incongruously rural-looking stone structure that was built in 1799 as a carriage house on what was then a twenty-three-acre estate owned by Abigail Adams Smith, daughter of John Adams, and her husband, Colonel William Stephens Smith. The estate and the surrounding area were called Mount Vernon after George Washington's home, and even now, built up as it is, the slope leading down to the East River along East 61st Street gives the name some credibility. The estate's main house burned in 1826, and the carriage house became the Mount Vernon Hotel, which served primarily as a day resort for short-distance travelers from the more heavily developed portion of Manhattan several miles to the south. Less than a decade later it reverted to private use and was the home of the Towle family for much of the rest of the nineteenth century. The Colonial Dames of America purchased the building in 1924 and renovated it; it opened as a museum in 1939, was designated a city landmark in 1967, and was placed on the National Register of Historic Places in 1973. The museum focuses on the building's brief period of use as an early nineteenth-century resort, when it was known for good food and genteel entertainment. Period rooms on display include a wonderfully detailed kitchen, which the docent who took me through the house described with particular enthusiasm, a delightful ladies' parlor, a surprisingly unadorned but apparently authentic bedroom (some guests did stay overnight or longer), and a gentlemen's parlor/gaming room adjacent to the Tavern Room. The museum is open Tuesday through Sunday from 11 AM to 4 PM; in 2002, adult admission was $4. There are also special events, such as December candlelight tours, holiday concerts, and an annual Washington's Birthday Ball geared toward families.

After a tour of the Mount Vernon Hotel Museum and Garden, you can head west a couple of blocks to **Bloomingdale's** (1000 Third Avenue, between Lexington and Third Avenues, 59th and 60th Streets, 212-705-2000; www.bloomingdales.com) if you are in the mood to browse and shop. Although there are many Bloomingdale's branches in the suburbs, for a teenager who's grown up with malls, the concept of a store that takes up a whole city block and has elevators and escalators galore is impressive. My daughter, Rebecca, and I made a trip to Bloomingdale's one spring weekday when there was no school because of a teachers' meeting. I had decades-old memories of the store's labyrinthine layout, and although some specifics have changed, the intriguing multiple levels and seemingly endless floor space survived. A friend of hers who had made the trip a few weeks earlier told Rebecca about the equally vast area on the second floor that sells clothes marketed to teenagers. As expected, Rebecca loved it, and she was equally impressed by the store's huge shoe department. As we were trying to figure out what color top would go with the colorful Free People rayon skirt she had selected, a well-groomed shopper, apparently in her sixties, advised us, in an expert's tone, that yellow would be great with the skirt. Sure enough, although yellow was the one color the skirt did not contain, it was indeed the color to wear with it, in the form of a clingy Michael Star three-quarter-sleeve pullover. It continues to be one of Rebecca's favorite school outfits.

As an added bonus for out-of-town day-trippers, Bloomingdale's is exceptionally easy to reach by subway from both Grand Central Terminal and Penn Station, since the 4, 5, and 6 (from Grand Central) and the N, R, and W (from Sixth Avenue and 34th Street, one block east of Penn Station) trains all stop at 59th Street and Lexington Avenue.

We had lunch that day at a **California Pizza Kitchen** (201 East 60th Street, 212-755-7773), which fit the bill perfectly for that particular day. The food was good enough, the prices reasonable by city standards, the service surprisingly friendly, and our table on the restaurant's upper level had a good view of the street below. If you want to keep your trip all under one roof, Bloomingdale's itself has a number of places to eat, including the 59th and Lex Café, the elegant Train Bleu, and the less-formal Forty Carrots.

If you enjoy small, specialized shops, another place you might want to explore is **Tender Buttons** (173 East 62nd Street, 212-758-7004), on a side street between Third and Lexington Avenues. I first heard about it from a colleague who used to work for a fashion magazine in New York. As its name (derived from a Gertrude Stein title) tells you, it is a place to find buttons of all sorts, from plain old shirt or coat buttons to elaborate fasteners of metal, wood, even ivory.

After exploring the Queensboro Bridge neighborhood, consider heading uptown along the eastern edges of the East Side. This could mean a walk or bus ride up First or York Avenues, with a stop or side-street detour somewhere in the 70s or 80s, as you mood takes you. If it's lunchtime or snack time, **Le Pain Quotidien** (1336 First Avenue between 71st and 72nd Streets, 212-717-4800) is an option worth considering. This Belgian bakery/restaurant chain has several outlets in Manhattan and serves very good, relatively reasonably priced breads, pastries, breakfasts, sandwiches, soups, and other treats.

When you reach 86th Street, turn east; the cluttered, commercial thoroughfare turns into a pleasant residential street with a treat at its eastern end. The **Henderson Place Historic District,** a tiny cul-de-sac that runs between 86th and 87th Streets parallel to York and East End Avenues, is lined with twenty-four pretty little town houses that seem to personify the romantic ideal of living on a small, intimate, picturesque street in the midst of a major city. The houses were built in the early 1880s; they were designed to make an attractive package, with turrets, gables, bay windows, and other architectural details that were considered delightfully quaint even in the nineteenth century. An equally distinctive row of buildings fronts on East End Avenue and runs between 86th and 87th Streets. Coming back to 86th Street and looking toward the East River, the view is blocked by a low but surprisingly rocky hill, the kind you see in Central Park and on parts of Riverside Drive. This is the western edge of **Carl Schurz Park,** a nice place to stroll and look out at the river. The pretty house in the park at 88th Street is **Gracie Mansion,** the former country house that now serves as the official residence of the mayor of New York City. Incidentally, **NY Waterway** (800-53-FERRY/533-3779) operates a commuter-ferry shuttle from the pier at 90th Street down to Pier 17 at Wall Street. Though the ferry runs primarily at rush hour, if you time things right it's also a fun way to get from one part of Manhattan to another.

Eighty-sixth Street is the heart of a neighborhood still known as Yorkville, which by the broadest definition runs from 72nd Street to 96th Street east of Fifth Avenue as far the East River. During the nineteenth century and through much of the twentieth century, the eastern half of the neighborhood was largely German, with substantial outposts of Hungarians and other European immigrants. Carl Schurz, after whom the neighborhood park is named, was a German immigrant who served as a general in the

Union army during the Civil War, was active in Republican Party politics, and later edited the *New York Post* and *Harper's Weekly*; he lived in Yorkville at various times. The blocks from Fifth Avenue to Park Avenue are part of the traditional, affluent Upper East Side. Some of the blocks from First Avenue to Lexington Avenue, especially in the upper 80s and into the 90s, have been taken over by twentysomethings who gather in the avenue's bars and restaurants, but there are still traces of the past tucked in among the cell phone stores.

Orwasher's Bakery (308 East 78th Street, 212-288-6569) is a survivor from an earlier era, and deserves to be. Its breads are delicious whether or not you remember eating breads just like them at your grandmother's house. The fact that it is tucked away on a quiet side street adds to its charm. Another specialty food shop that reflects the past while thriving in the present is the **Elk Candy Company** (1628 Second Avenue, 212-650-1177; www.elkcandy.com), established in 1933. It has nothing to do with elks, and everything to do with marzipan. My daughter, who likes both pigs and marzipan, was delighted by the little pink marzipan pigs I brought home from Elk. Colorfully realistic fruit, down-to-earth miniature potatoes, and other shapes, all made of marzipan, are also available; so are chocolate candies.

This neighborhood has so many restaurants that it's hard to walk down even a single block without stopping to read menus and deciding that you are hungry. But if you want a specific destination, here is one suggestion. A few blocks and a continent away from Orwasher's Bakery, is **Pig Heaven** (1540 Second Avenue, between 80th and 81st Streets, 212-744-4333), a Chinese restaurant. The name alone is enough to delight children, and the food should please all ages. **Heidelberg** (1648 Second Avenue, between 85th and 86th Streets, 212-628-2332) is the last of Yorkville's traditional German restaurants.

8

Central Park:
Not Just for People Who
Can Walk Home from There

■ ■ ■ ■ ■ ■ ■ ■ ■ ■

Of course Central Park has all the basics of a park, like trees, fields, and flowers. With more than twenty playgrounds and lots of open space for running, jumping, and playing catch, it's a wonderful place to bring children. It's also a place where adults can enjoy all the activities you expect to enjoy in a park, from tennis to nature walks. And it's a place where, to avoid bikers, in-line skaters, and even equestrians, you have to cross pathways and roadways almost as carefully as you do busy city streets. Open-air opera, softball games, rock group reunions, and playgrounds all have their moments here. What truly makes Central Park special, though, even beyond the dazzling warm-weather entertainment and the picture-perfect views it presents, is the overall sense of place you get when you stand near any edge of the park and look north, south, east, or west.

Central Park is bounded on the east by Fifth Avenue, on the west by Central Park West (which is Eighth Avenue south of the park and Frederick Douglass Boulevard north of the park), on the south by Central Park South, otherwise known as 59th Street, and on the north by Central Park North, which is really 110th Street. The grid pattern of numbered streets is a wonderful thing when it comes to figuring out where you are within the park, since the transverses and entrances were all keyed to numbered cross streets. When you look at a map of Manhattan, it turns out that Central Park is truly central, despite having been developed when the population of Manhattan was concentrated well south of what is now Central Park South.

The landscape, naturally beautiful as it appears, is not natural. Central Park was built on the site of a more miscellaneous landscape that was home to hundreds of people, scattered in a number of small settlements, including Seneca Village, a black community containing churches and a school as well as homes. The park was designed a few years before the Civil War by Frederick Olmsted and Calvert Vaux, who in 1857 won a design competition run by the newly created Central Park Commission. The goal was to create a picturesque landscape with unobstructed views. Countless trees and shrubs were planted and tons of earth moved to create hills and make way for lakes and ponds. Carriage drives, walkways, and equestrian paths crossed each other over dozens of bridges; four below-grade roadways carried crosstown traffic without disturbing the views. There have been changes and modifications to the park over the years, but the overall effect hasn't been altered in any major way.

Central Park

Bridge, Central Park

Among the defining landscape features of the park are the open spaces, such as the Sheep Meadow and the Great Lawn, and the rustic areas, such as the Ramble. The **Sheep Meadow,** between 66th and 69th Streets closer to the west side of the park, was planned as space for military exercises and was, literally, converted to a sheep meadow, home to 150 sheep in the 1860s. The sheep left in 1934, but the open space remained. It's a designated quiet zone, dedicated to picnicking, kite flying, and other relatively low-key, low-decibel activities. The **Great Lawn,** between 81st and 85th Streets in the middle of the park, on the site of a reservoir that was drained in 1929, is essentially a giant playing field behind the Metropolitan Museum of Art. The **Ramble** is one of the park's original design elements. Located in mid-park between 74th and 79th Streets, it's hilly, with winding paths and wooded slopes, and, although beautiful, has a reputation for being a place best visited in daylight and with other people.

The park is also full of buildings, fountains, bridges, and statues that add to its distinctive charm. **Belvedere Castle,** built in 1872 as a pavilion from which to look out over what was then Croton Reservoir, now looks out over the Great Lawn and over Belvedere Lake, which is a small reminder of the old reservoir. The **Delacorte Theatre,** home of the New York Shakespeare Festival, is nearby (see chapter 14). **Bethesda Fountain**— mid-park at 72nd Street—dates to 1873 and is dedicated to Civil War soldiers who died at sea. The stone staircase that leads down to it is one of those famous New York places that you probably recognize from movies. The recently refurbished **Dairy** (mid-park at 65th Street, 212-794-6564) is an ornate building described by the Central Park Conservancy as part Swiss chalet and part Gothic country church. Whatever stylistic terms are applied to it, it is delightful, with an open section made of wood and a closed section of granite. It now serves as a visitor information center and recreation building, open Tuesday through Sunday from 10 AM to 5 PM (4 PM in winter). It really was a dairy once; the idea was that city children of the mid-nineteenth century could go to the Dairy in the Park with their families and stop to get a glass of fresh, clean milk. Not far from the Dairy there's a rocky outcropping called the Kinderberg, with a pergola housing two dozen chess tables.

The elegant bridges that dot the park combine function with charm and reflect Olmsted and Vaux's original vision of the place. **Bow Bridge,** which crosses Belvedere Lake and leads to the Ramble, is one of the best-known, not just for the elegant cast-iron bridge itself but because of its setting. Among the memorable statues are **Alice in Wonderland,** near the eastern edge of the park at 75th Street, and **Balto,** on the east side of the park

Bethesda Fountain, Central Park

between 66th and 67th Streets, near the Delacorte Clock and the Tisch Children's Zoo. Balto was a sled dog who carried medicine during a 1925 Alaskan diphtheria epidemic.

So what can you actually do in the park once you have finished admiring it, gotten slightly lost walking through a section of it, or found your way to a playground or comfortable bench for a brief rest? (Keep in mind that this chapter is just an introduction, intended to invite you to explore the park rather than provide a complete overview of it.) The fact that there are so many things to see in the Park means that a visit there can be a walking tour, during which you look at what interests you and then go on to something else. But there are also specific attractions to consider ahead of time.

A trip to the zoo is an obvious choice, especially if you are accompanied by children. Central Park provides a magical setting, and people who grew up in New York more than two or three decades ago probably remember visits to the zoo as special childhood treats. The **Central Park Wildlife Center** (Fifth Avenue at 64th Street, 212-439-6500) is small and cozy. The Wildlife Conservation Society took the old Central Park Zoo over in 1984 and essentially rebuilt it as a state-of-the art facility that highlights conservation and gives visitors an opportunity to observe wildlife from tropical, temperate, and polar zones. The polar bears are playful and the Sea Lion Pool is deservedly legendary. Seal feeding times are 11:30 AM, 2 PM, and 4 PM, and people still crowd around to watch the seals jump for their food. There are benches in the perennial garden that surrounds the pool, and there's a café nearby, so you don't have to go hungry once the seals are fed.

For families, a don't-miss feature of the zoo is the newly refurbished **Tisch Children's Zoo** north of the main zoo. At its interactive exhibits, visitors get the chance to touch sheep, a cow, and other farm animals, including a Vietnamese pot-bellied pig. You can buy food to feed the animals. In addition to the live animals, there are small sculptures outside the animal pens that make lifelike sounds when touched. There's an Enchanted Forest with an aviary and make-believe oak. The zoo also has two children's theaters, where shows about animals are performed.

The Central Park Wildlife Center is open daily year-round, with slightly shorter hours November through March. Admission is $3.50 for adults, $1.25 for senior citizens, and 50 cents for children age three to twelve.

Even if you don't want to stop at the zoo you may want to see the **George Delacorte Musical Clock,** which stands between the Wildlife Center and the Children's Zoo. This colorful clock, mounted on brick arches, plays nursery rhymes every hour on the hour while musical creatures—including a bear with a tambourine, a hippopotamus with a violin, and a penguin with drum—move around the base and two monkeys at the top of the clock look as though they are striking a bell. There are shorter "performances" on the half hour.

Anyone who has read E. B. White's *Stuart Little* (or has seen the movie) will remember the model sailboats. They sail on the **Conservatory Water,** on the east side of the park between 72nd and 75th Streets. The season runs from spring through fall (generally, April through October), and people bring all sorts of models powered by radio or wind. For permit information, call 212-360-8133; model boats are available for sale or rent from Central Park Sailboats (917-796-1382). It's also fun to watch and admire.

If you want to get out on the water yourself, head for the nearby **Loeb Boathouse** (East Park Drive, north of 72nd Street, 212-517-2233). Tucked along the eastern arm of the lake, this is the place to rent a dinghy and row off into the sunset. Bicycle rentals are also available. The boathouse is open daily March through October, weather permitting. The waterside **Boathouse Café,** also open March through October, is a convenient place to stop for refreshment even if you aren't planning a bicycle or boat ride. The restaurant is open for lunch and dinner, the cafeteria for breakfast and lunch.

Another classic Central Park image is the **Friedsam Memorial Carousel** (about halfway between Fifth Avenue and Central Park West, at 64th Street; for more information, call 212-879-0244), the fourth carousel to occupy the site. Earlier ones burned, and this one was rescued from a trolley barn at Coney Island. It dates to 1908 and has 58 painted horses. It is open daily from 10 AM to 6 PM April through November; it is open on weekends from 10 AM to 4:30 PM, weather permitting, November through April.

Central Park is also a skater's paradise. In-line skaters can zoom along the pathways in all seasons, and there are also two skating rinks in the park. The **Wollman Memorial Rink** (east side of the park between 62nd and 63rd Streets, 212-396-1010) is crowded, famous, and easily accessible from midtown. There's an admission fee, and skate rental costs extra. Ice skating usually runs from mid-October through March, with in-line skating the rest of the year. The **Lasker Pool and Rink** (near East Drive between 107th and 108th Streets, 212-534-7639) is near the northern tip of the park, just below the Harlem Meer. Ice skating runs from November through March, and skate rentals are available. The rink turns into a pool on July 1.

A more contemplative seasonal destination is the **Shakespeare Garden** (West Park Drive and the 79th Street transverse). As the name suggests, its focus is on plants mentioned in Shakespeare's works. The spring bulb display is spectacular, and in June there's a lovely array of antique roses. Like the Sheep Meadow, this is an official quiet zone, and there are benches along the garden paths, making this a pleasant spot to catch your breath, literally and figuratively.

▦   ▦   ▦

From May through Labor Day, open-air concerts are a key part of the park's image and appeal. I used to love the feeling of walking out of the park after a concert and reentering the real world on Central Park West as part of a densely packed crowd of well-behaved people. Perhaps the best-known performance traditions are the free presentations on the Great Lawn by the **Metropolitan Opera** and the **New York Philharmonic**. There are also classical concerts at the **Naumburg Bandshell**, on the east side of the park at 70th Street. Also during the summer, the Central Park Conservancy hosts the **Harlem Meer Performance Festival** (212-860-1370), which features blues, jazz, salsa, and gospel music, and, like the Great Lawn events, is free. If you'd like to spend a musical evening in the park, check the Central Park Conservancy Web site (www.centralparknyc.org) and newspaper and magazine event listings.

Taking an organized tour run by the Central Park Conservancy and led by a volunteer is a great way to get to know the park in more detail. The free tours, which run from April through December, are especially suitable for both adults and children aged ten and older. Among the regularly scheduled walking tours in 2002 were "Views from the Past," starting at the Dairy and focusing on the history of the park; "The Castle and Its Kingdom," a walk around Belvedere Castle; and Saturday tours of the Conservatory Garden (on the east side of the park between 104th and 106th Streets), led by a curator of the six-acre garden. For more information about walking tours of Central Park, call 212-360-2726.

The park is full of places to eat: ice-cream carts, hot-dog vendors, food stands near the entrances, and several cafés. The star attraction, however, is Tavern on the Green, which occupies the site of the former sheepfold west of the Sheep Meadow. **Tavern on the Green** (Central Park West between 66th and 67th Streets, 212-873-3200) is an event restaurant, the kind you make reservations for and get dressed up for. It doesn't necessarily fit into a day trip to the park, but it might well be worth a trip in its own right for a festive event.

Central Park is so large, literally stretching for miles, that it has its own distinct neighborhoods, and it's hard to see it all in a single visit. (For more about the northern sections of Central Park, see chapter 12, "Upper Fifth Avenue: Not Just Hospitals.") Depending upon where in the park you want to go, there are several means of public transportation to use. Coming from Penn Station, you can take the C train to any one of several stops along Central Park West, then enter the park from there, or take the subway to 66th Street and take the crosstown bus if you want to get to the East Side. Similarly, if you are coming into the city via Grand Central Terminal, it's easy to take the 4, 5, or 6 train and get off at whichever Lexington Avenue stop is convenient for you, then walk west the three short blocks to the east side of the park. If you are coming by car, the parking garage at the Metropolitan Museum is an ideal place from which to begin your park exploration.

9

The Upper West Side: Everything for Everyone

When my suburban streets seem too uneventful and unpeopled, I enjoy taking a quick trip to the city by myself, whether to admire brownstones, visit a museum, or buy food. It's exercise, errand-running, and recreation. The Upper West Side, particularly the stretch from West 68th Street to about 89th Street, lends itself to all these pursuits. The side streets are full of brownstones, the avenues each have their own iconography, from the palatial apartment buildings, dignified cultural institutions, and wonderful views (and Central Park access) along Central Park West to the bustle of Broadway. There's Amsterdam Avenue, still occasionally a little forbidding, Columbus Avenue, looking like a cross between a *Friends* set and a casual-restaurant heaven, and West End Avenue, with its canyons of doorman buildings. Riverside Drive, with beautiful buildings and incredibly romantic and lovely vistas of the Hudson River and the Palisades, has its own appeal.

If the trains are running well, a weekday morning walk almost anywhere on the Upper West Side is an easy, spur-of-the-moment jaunt for me: an NJ Transit train will get me to Penn Station in half an hour. The Upper West Side is an easy trip for many suburbanites who live on train lines going into Penn Station or who take buses to the Port Authority Bus Terminal on West 42nd Street. Even from Grand Central Terminal, it's not a hard trip; the M104 bus, after all, makes its often slow way west on 42nd Street and then up Broadway.

The Upper West Side is really a mix-and-match destination with something for everyone. When I think of my own landmarks, a variety of unrelated places come to mind, among them **Murder Ink** (2486 Broadway, between 92nd and 93rd Streets, 212-362-8905), for paradoxically escapist reading material; **Tip Top Shoes** (155 West 72nd Street, 800-WALK-ING/925-5464; www.tiptopshoes.com), where I bought my first Mephistos and discovered that leather walking shoes do indeed last much longer than sneakers; and **Barney Greengrass** (541 Amsterdam Avenue, between 86th and 87th Streets, 212-724-4707), for a deliberately nostalgic atmosphere as well as borscht and smoked fish. Yes, many of the stores throughout the Upper West Side reflect the retail chains that exist throughout the country, and some blocks bear every resemblance to your local mall except that they are sunny or rainy, windswept or muggy, rather than indoors and perfectly climate-controlled. Still, when you come cross a Talbot's, Gap, or L'Occitane in a new and cosmopolitan setting, the overall ambience is distinctive. The food, in fact, may be worth the journey by itself, whether you bring it home or find your way to a quintessentially urban restaurant, traditional Chinese, unfamiliar small ethnic, or glossy new Asian hybrid.

And then there are the museums. The American Museum of Natural History. The New-York Historical Society. The Children's Museum of Manhattan. Obviously, the last of these doesn't have quite the sweeping appeal of the first two, but if you are a four-year-old, or a four-year-old's parent, it's a good place to know about.

Back when we lived on West 68th Street, Columbus Avenue was well on the way to gentrification and transformation, but Amsterdam Avenue hadn't begun its metamorphosis, and the Rose Center for Earth and Space wasn't even a twinkle in an architect's eye. We took the crowds, clutter, and abundance of the local Fairway market for granted. We didn't return to the neighborhood much except for the occasional foray to the American Museum of Natural History to break up a Sunday afternoon and entertain our children.

There was a time, a long time ago, when the **American Museum of Natural History** (Central Park West at 79th Street, 212-769-5100; www.amnh.org) was the main reason people traveled to the Upper West Side, either from other parts of the city or from places outside the city. Since the nineteenth century, the museum has been a majestic presence on Central

Park West and a rather hulking, somehow less majestic one on Columbus Avenue; although many galleries have been refurbished in recent years, and the Rose Center for Earth and Space has dazzled the planetarium-going public in the last couple of years, the museum has not yet become one of those brightly lit, button-pressing child-oriented science palaces, like Boston's Museum of Science and the Liberty Science Center. Galleries continue to be renovated, reopening with modern bells and whistles (in other words, computers and videos) as well as the original items that made the museum what it is in the first place. You can still find marble stairways, not-quite-bright-hallways, and the wonderful dark caverns housing the fascinating, vivid dioramas—not entirely politically correct anymore since they presumably reflect the killing of the hundreds of wild creatures now on display thanks to skilled taxidermy.

The Museum of Natural History is a classic family destination now, just as it was fifteen years ago when my children were the right age to be taken there on a rainy Sunday, and just as it was decades before that when I saw the giant dinosaur skeleton in the Theodore Roosevelt Rotunda—that is, the entrance hall—for the first time.

The museum was established shortly after the Civil War, and President Ulysses S. Grant attended the groundbreaking ceremony for the present building in 1874. The tradition of extraordinary taxidermy displays dates back to the 1880s. The museum sponsored paleontology expeditions throughout the early twentieth century. The name Roy Chapman Andrews appeared constantly in the dinosaur books I used to read aloud to my son; Andrews's expeditions to Mongolia were among the many explorations the museum has sponsored over the past century. It's not surprising, then, that there are three impressive dinosaur halls at the museum, as well as Hall of Fossil Mammals. Computers have arrived at the museum, and visitors can expand their knowledge and imaginations via interactive stations, but for many people, the greatest attraction of a trip to the museum continues to be the fossils and artifacts and the tremendous geographical and chronological scope of the exhibits.

The museum's Discovery Room is geared specifically to visitors aged five to twelve. Its puzzles, games, and artifacts provide children with a behind-the-scenes look at the various fields of science covered by the museum's exhibits and programs. One highlight is a replica of an African baobab tree, complete with tropical birds, insects, and other creatures. There's also a Kwakiutl totem pole, a cast skeleton of a fourteen-foot dinosaur, an assortment of fossils, and other items to pique the interest of elementary-schoolers.

Accessible as it is to children, there are always pleasures for adults at the museum. For example, the new gem display is exciting for children because the minerals are shiny and colorful, but it is also a visual delight for older visitors, and the multilevel layout adds to its appeal. The special exhibits cut across generational lines, too. Several years ago, a show devoted to diamonds was a great success, combining serious information about diamond mining with displays of amazingly lavish craftsmanship and almost priceless jewelry. More recently, the museum did much the same thing for pearls and for baseball (yes, baseball, with a spring 2002 exhibit that included items lent by the Baseball Hall of Fame in Cooperstown).

The legendary Hayden Planetarium opened in 1935. Everyone who grew up in or near New York City from the 1940s through the 1980s probably remembers stepping on the scales in the hallway outside the auditorium to find out how his or her weight on the moon, on Jupiter, and on other planets, compared to "real" weight on Earth. The new Hayden Planetarium Space Theater is part of the **Rose Center for Earth and Space**, whose three-story glass structure rises dramatically next to the more traditional mass of the museum. Below ground level, the Dorothy and Lewis B. Cullman Hall of the Universe focuses on modern astrophysics, with zones devoted to the universe, stars, galaxies, and planets. The first-floor David S. and Ruth L. Gottesman Hall of Planet Earth has varied attractions, including rock samples and video displays of events such as earthquakes and volcanic eruptions. The visually striking second floor includes the Scales of the Universe Walkway, Big Bang exhibit, and the Harriet and Robert Heilbrunn Cosmic Pathway. The Space Theater, home of the Space Show, is on the top floor; this is where you get to see the twenty-first-century version of the seemingly three-dimensional Hayden sky, thanks to the Zeiss Mark IX Star Projector and Digital Dome Projection System.

You can buy tickets just to the Rose Center or purchase combination tickets to the Rose Center, Space Show, and museum. The Rose Center is open Sunday through Thursday 10 AM to 5:45 PM and Friday and Saturday until 8:45 PM. It is closed on Christmas and Thanksgiving.

The American Museum of Natural History is a huge place; you can manage to get lost in its corridors, especially if one of your personal landmark exhibits is closed for renovation or it's no longer as you remember it because it's been redone. The halls sometimes echo with the sound of stroller wheels and parent-child conversations. There are several places to eat or snack, the largest of which is the Museum Food Court on the museum's lower level; here you can choose from a wide range of offerings, including salads, pizza, sushi, and sandwiches. The adjacent Big Dipper Ice Cream Café is what it sounds like, and there are other spots throughout the museum, including an outdoor café.

If you drive to the city, there is a parking garage at the museum; street parking is at a premium in the neighborhood, although it's not unheard of to get lucky and find a parking spot, especially on a summer weekend. You can also reach the museum easily by public transportation. The 81st Street station of the B and C subway lines is adjacent to the basement level of the museum—you never even walk outside after leaving the platform. The M10 bus, which goes up Eighth Avenue, stopping both behind Penn Station and in front of the Port Authority Bus Terminal, will take you right to the museum's front entrance on Central Park West. The M104 bus, which you can board right outside Grand Central Terminal, will take you to Broadway and 79th Street, where you can walk east to the museum. Or you can get a free bus transfer to the 79th Street crosstown bus (M79), which you can take to 81st Street and Central Park West—an appealing idea if you have small children, the weather is particularly inclement, or you want to save your energies for walking in the museum itself.

At the corner of Central Park West, just across 77th Street from the south side of the American Museum of Natural History, stands the **New York Historical Society** (2 West 77th Street, 212-873-3400; www.nyhistory.org), another of those perfect rainy-day destinations that is also interesting enough to visit in good weather. Although it is much smaller and more manageable than the natural history museum, a visit to either one is enough for a day trip. Founded in 1804, the New-York Historical Society offers exhibits that generally focus on American life and history as reflected by New York experience. Its collection includes everything from paintings and photographs to chairs and china, as well as an extensive research library—the oldest in the country.

The New-York Historical Society has changed over the years, with the most dramatic development being the creation of the dazzling Henry Luce III Center for the Study of American Culture. This might be described as a fantasy family attic, if your family had an unparalleled collection of early-

American furniture, campaign buttons, George Washington memorabilia, Tiffany lamps, and hundreds of other prized artifacts of American life. Unlike the contents of most attics, however, these items are displayed in a well-lit, well-organized series of halls, accented by informative placards and the occasional computer. Much as I used to enjoy visiting the New-York Historical Society in its earlier incarnation—the fire engines on the ground floor were a great favorite in my own school-trip days—I think the displays at the Luce Center may be even more enjoyable.

Last time I visited the museum, early on a weekday afternoon in early 2002, it was more crowded than I had ever seen it. On the first floor, where a gallery displayed September 11 photographs taken by members of the Magnum photographers' collective, a silent video of the airplanes flying into the World Trade Center was playing continuously, and people were standing in front of the screen transfixed and silent, except for the gasps that followed the sight of the explosion caused by the second airplane. It wasn't the mood usually associated with the museum, but it was certainly part of New York history and experience. When this book went to press, the New-York Historical Society continued to focus on various aspects of the attacks and their aftermath in its "History Responds" project. The museum also presents a variety of other special exhibits on everything from the Thanksgiving Day parade to New York–based family businesses to complement its wonderfully satisfying permanent displays. It also offers an appealing array of programs for children and families, featuring such diverse historical landmarks as Nathan Hale, a real-life spy/hero; Felicity, of American Girl book/doll fame; cabbies; vaudeville; and nineteenth-century games. In addition, in the permanent Kids' Corner, there is a child-size re-creation of Broadway between 82nd and 83rd Streets in 1901. This miniature piece of the past includes a food market, a bakery, and an apartment.

The New-York Historical Society is open Tuesday through Sunday from 10 AM to 5 PM; admission is $5 for adults and $3 for children and senior citizens.

If you yearn for more history after visiting the New-York Historical Society, you might consider a bus ride (the M79 cross-town to Riverside Drive, where you can transfer to the M104) uptown to **Grant's Tomb** (Riverside Drive and 122nd Street, 212-666-1640; www.nps.gov/gegr). This massive memorial to President and Civil

War General Ulysses S. Grant was dedicated in 1897, more than a decade after Grant's death. It has an extraordinary view of the Hudson River and serves as an impressive landmark on a windswept corner a few blocks northwest of Columbia University. It is administered by the National Park Service and is open daily from 9 AM to 5 PM.

Riverside Church, with its imposing tower, world's largest carillon, and ornate stonework, is just down the street, at the corner of Riverside Drive and 120th Street. The even larger **Cathedral Church of St. John the Divine** (1047 Amsterdam Avenue at 112th Street, 212-316-7540; www.stjohnthedivine.org) is a brisk, varied walk south and east across the Columbia campus. Both these impressive houses of worship sponsor a variety of concerts and special events for the public in addition to their religious services.

For the very young, there's the **Children's Museum of Manhattan** (the Tisch Building, 212 West 83rd Street, 212-721-1234; www.cmom.org): a visit here is a selfless act for parents, given how universally interesting the two big West Side museums are for anyone over the age of five or six. (Coincidentally, the Children's Museum of Manhattan is just east of the Broadway block that is re-created in miniature at the New-York Historical Society.) The Children's Museum of Manhattan offers a rich variety of exhibitions and programs for the preschool/kindergarten set. For example, in 2001 it featured "Arthur's™ World," a traveling exhibition based on Marc Brown's delightful and very popular picture books, and one of its special 2002 exhibits was "Where the Wild Things Are: Maurice Sendak in His Own Words and Pictures." Permanent exhibits include "Sleds, Skateboards and Scooters: From the Alex Shear Collection" and "WordPlay." The former, as its title suggests, displays children's modes of transportation (albeit antiques that they cannot touch), and the second is essentially a language-development play area that includes colorful attractions like the Chatterbug Tree. The museum's regular hours are Wednesday through Sunday from 10 AM to 5 PM. Admission is $6 for adults and children; children under one year are admitted free.

It may seem a little silly in the land of mall-sized supermarkets and over-stocked kitchens to go to New York to buy food, but this isn't just any food. The bagels at **H&H** (2239 Broadway at 80th Street, 212-595-8003) are reputedly among the best in the city. Although some people find the bagels too big and soft, they're family favorites in our household, and when we stop by, we stock up on at least a dozen, enjoying some when we get home and freezing the rest. There's a large West 46th Street branch near the Hudson River (639 West 46th Street at Twelfth Avenue, 212-595-8000), where the bagels are made for shipping as well as sale onsite but the location doesn't lend itself to a casual drop-in unless you happen to be visiting the *Intrepid* nearby (see chapter 13).

Of course once you have your H&H bagels, you will certainly want to make a stop at **Zabar's** (2245 Broadway, between 80th and 81st Streets, 212-787-2000; www.zabars.com). Zabar's is legendary but not scary, busy but usually not overwhelming, famous but not fancy. Although some of the things to be found on its shelves are also available elsewhere, such as chocolate-truffle cakes from Desserts by David Glass and colorful jars of Sarabeth's preserves, I don't know of any suburban food store that begins to match the variety and ambience of this store—even without considering the kitchen-equipment offerings on the mezzanine. The classic image of Zabar's is probably the fish counter, where people take numbers, then wait surprisingly patiently to order all sorts of smoked fish, not just the familiar lox and less-salty smoked salmon but sable, whitefish, and more. The entrance door opens on an enticing cheese section whose shelves and coolers offer an international tour of dairy products often at more reasonable prices than our local supermarkets can manage. Explore the store's corners and aisles for prepared food, coffee beans, breads, jams, and packaged foods.

H&H and Zabar's are reason enough to make the trip to the neighborhood, but there are other food-related attractions, notably **Fairway Market** (2127 Broadway at 74th Street, 212-595-1880) and **Citarella** (2135 Broadway at 75th Street, 212-874-0383; www.citarella.com). Fairway was a glorified produce-plus stand in the 1970s when I lived nearby; it still sells produce but is perhaps even better known for cheeses. It gets very crowded and has a traffic pattern that makes it seems crowded under almost any circumstances, but it's fun to visit, though you may be glad you don't have to shop there regularly. (There is a larger branch far uptown, at 2328 Twelfth Avenue at 133rd Street, 212-234-3883.) Citarella started out as a fish market and continues to sell lots of fish but has branched out in the usual ways, selling meat and prepared foods. As you wander up and down Broadway, you will find many other stores, including supermarkets and relatively unadorned produce stands, but not all will stand out to the eye or mind. One establishment that should call out to you is **Neuhaus Chocolate** (2151 Broadway near 75th Street, 212-712-2112), a gracious enclave on a busy block. It is worth giving into temptation here. The boxed chocolates are a fine choice if you are in a hurry, but it's even better to choose your own selections from the display counter at the back of the store; the chocolates, which taste as good as they look, are sold by weight, so you can put together exactly the right combination in whatever quantity you want.

If you prefer to punctuate museum visits and neighborhood strolls with a stop at a restaurant, the problem is not finding a place but choosing one from among so many. As long as you have cash or a credit card with you, it's hard to go hungry on the Upper West Side at any time of day or night. One relative newcomer likely to require advance planning—that is, a reservation—is **Ruby Foo's** (2182 Broadway at 77th Street, 212-724-6700). Like the theater-district Ruby Foo's, this is a highly decorated destination restaurant that also happens to serve excellent Asian food and very tempting cross-cultural desserts. The West Side **EJ's Luncheonette** (447 Amsterdam Avenue between 81st and 82nd Streets, 212-873-3444), like its crosstown and downtown siblings, is an informal, unchallenging place to go for familiar food.

On any given block, especially along Columbus and Amsterdam Avenues, the restaurant choices seem boundless. The neighborhood from Lincoln Center to Columbia University abounds in Chinese, Thai, and Vietnamese restaurants, Latin American spots, and a generous sprinkling of almost every other nationality. There's also the idiosyncratic Upper Broadway Cuban-Chinese amalgam. Two appealing Southeast Asian places are **River** (345 Amsterdam Avenue, between 76th and 77th Streets, 212-579-1888), which combines Thai and Vietnamese offerings, and **Penang** (240 Columbus Avenue at 71st Street, 212-769-3988), part of a small Malaysian chain. **Gray's Papaya** (2090 Broadway at 72nd Street, 212-799-0243, across from the 72nd Street subway station), is locally famous, though it may not look like the kind of place you think you should stop at. In its own way, it's excellent; even better, it continues to be as affordable as it was decades ago when it was my neighborhood fast-food stop.

Lincoln Center

Lincoln Center (212-LINCOLN/546-2656; www.lincolncenter.org) isn't the kind of place you decide to pop into spontaneously because it has just occurred to you that you would like to spend a few hours at the opera. The sight of the dignified white buildings of the performing-arts complex, which extends from 62nd Street to 66th Street and is bounded on the east by Broadway and Columbus Avenue and on the west by Amsterdam Avenue, is very impressive. The soaring central fountain and the endless streams of people crossing the plaza may make you want to be part of the mini-world encircled and symbolized by the concert halls, but time and ticket availability may not allow for a last-minute decision to attend an event. All the same, Lincoln Center can be a great day (or evening) trip destination, and it doesn't necessarily take a lot of planning or much more money than attending a cultural event anywhere else. In addition to the Metropolitan Opera House and Avery Fisher Hall (home of the New York Philharmonic, which also plays at Carnegie Hall), venues include the New York State Theater (home

Lincoln Center

of the New York City Ballet and, at this writing, of the New York City Opera), Vivian Beaumont Theater, Mitzi E. Newhouse Theater, and Alice Tully Hall. Performances at the various locations include not only operas and symphonies but also chamber music, dance, theater, and more. There are also open-air concerts and festivals, even free concerts at the Guggenheim Bandshell, mostly in the summer. Each winter for a month or so, the Big Apple Circus sets up tent in Damrosch Park, south of the Metropolitan Opera House. Taking children to the Big Apple Circus makes for a wonderful excursion, since the circus performers are dazzlingly skilled while the setting is small enough to provide some semblance of intimacy no matter where you sit.

Lincoln Center is easy to get to by subway (take the 1 or 9 train to 66th Street) and bus (M104 along Broadway or M11 up Amsterdam or down Columbus), taxi drivers know where it is, and for if you are driving, there are two underground parking garages right on the premises, so transportation is not a concern.

Sometimes the idea of going to Lincoln Center is better than the reality, but sometimes the reality is every bit as good as the fantasy. Several years ago my husband decided he wanted to discover opera at Lincoln Center, so we bought the cheapest possible Saturday-night subscription and arranged our schedule for the next several months to allow for periodic excursions into the city. Beautiful as the music was, we didn't like knowing we had to go on a specific night, without fail, several times in a row. About a year later, he decided to splurge on a single good seat at a Saturday-afternoon performance of *La Bohème,* which he had never seen. That trip was a great success, partly because he had purchased the ticket by telephone only days before, providing an extra dash of adventure to this particular excursion. And that was a great day trip for him: a short drive into the city, parking at the Lincoln Center garage, hours of sitting in a pricey but excellent orchestra seat, and the chance to hear and see one of the most beautiful and timeless operas performed on a world-class stage. It was memorable and well worth the money, and the experience is readily transferred to any venue at Lincoln Center. A perfect recital at Alice Tully Hall, a symphony concert at Avery Fisher Hall; all it takes is planning and money.

Naturally, going to Lincoln Center, like any other day trip to the Upper West Side, is likely to involve a meal either before or after the event. The possibilities are so abundant that it seems arbitrary and almost futile to single any out; still, there are a few universal favorites that my family, like many others, has enjoyed over the years. If you don't have your own favorites and don't want to go too far afield, here are a few suggestions. With children, whether you are there in the neighborhood for the circus or a seasonal performance of *The Nutcracker,* **Café Fiorello** (1900 Broadway between 63rd and 64th Street, 212-595-5330) is a good choice. It's also fine for grownups without children, but the relaxed atmosphere, crayons-for-kids place settings, and crisp, cute, individual pizzas make it particularly child-friendly. Another child-friendly option is **John's Pizzeria** (48 West 65th Street, 212-721-7001). **Shun Lee** (43 West 65th Street between Columbus Avenue and Central Park West, 212-595-8895) is relatively expensive and formal, but it's also very good. My son developed an affection for its dumplings when he was in high school and visiting a summer-camp friend who lived on Riverside Drive; he's out of college now and still advocates going to Shun Lee on family outings so he can have the same dumplings. The menu goes far beyond the (unarguably delicious) dumplings though. Down the price and sophistication scale, the Lincoln Center–area branch of **Ollie's** (1991 Broadway near 67th Street, 212-595-8181) is a reliable option for Chinese noodle dishes, dumplings, soups, and similar offerings, especially if your time is limited or you are accompanied by hungry children. **Rosa Mexicano** (51 Columbus Avenue a 62nd Street, 212-977-7700) is a branch of a popular East Side Mexican restaurant; the guacamole, made at your table, is a star attraction.

10

Great Manhattan Museums: Big and Small, Crowds and All

■ ■ ■ ■ ■ ■ ■ ■ ■

People come from all over the world to visit our museums, just as we travel thousands of miles to see the Louvre, the British Museum, and all those others that seem all the more glamorous and civilized because they are far from home. Although New York's great museums are part of tourist lore, those of us lucky enough to live close to the city have the advantage of being able to visit them at a leisurely pace, as the mood strikes and schedules allow.

It's amazing how many New York museums are within walking distance of each other. On the Upper East Side, there are so many, and their presence is so much a part of the area's identity, that the street signs on Fifth Avenue from 79th Street to 104th Street identify that stretch of the avenue as Museum Mile. The trouble is, of course, that even if you choose a day when at least one museum is open late, there's just too much to see. You could spend an entire day at some of the museums, and a full morning or afternoon at others. Without even leaving the neighborhood, you can slip into the Jewish Museum, the Cooper-Hewitt, the Whitney, the Guggenheim, Frick, or the Metropolitan. And that's not the end of the possibilities. The Museum of the City of New York is still a mainstay of Upper Fifth Avenue, and on the next block, the Museo Del Barrio also beckons.

The **Metropolitan Museum of Art** (Fifth Avenue at 82nd Street, 212-535-7710; www.metmuseum.org) is often the starting point for a discovery of New York museums. How could it not be? It stretches for blocks on the west side of Fifth Avenue, backing onto Central Park. It has an amazingly convenient parking garage that provides direct access to the museum. The 79th Street crosstown bus (M79) stops a block from its front door, and if you are coming from uptown, you get real front-door service, because the Fifth Avenue bus (M1, M2, or M4) stops right there. You can approach the museum from Central Park after a leisurely walk through urban meadows, or from an elegant East Eighties side street. Arriving at the museum is in itself one of the ultimate New York City experiences. Going inside is even better. From the array of people sitting on the massive front steps to the multiple languages you hear from fellow visitors, everything about a trip to this museum feels like an event. It's a legendary place, a giant of the art museum world, built in a grand architectural style, and it feels as well as looks the part.

I remember going there as a high-school student from Westchester County to see suits of armor and buy postcards to use in a project about *Ivanhoe,* the sort of thing that nowadays we'd call multimedia and create

The Metropolitan Museum of Art

using PowerPoint; I typed the project and used the postcards as illustrations. I also especially remember a snowy Lincoln's Birthday trip, years later, to the museum to see an Impressionist exhibit with the man who is now my husband. The museum was open, both our offices were closed, and the city was quiet but not shut down by a snowfall—something between a blizzard and a snow shower.

The nice thing about being able to make short, multiple trips to the museum is that you don't have to see everything all at once. You can take your children to the massive arms and armor room, or let a budding music student admire the musical instruments on display nearby. You can treat yourself to an afternoon of admiring thirteenth-century religious art, Greek statues, or some of each. The seemingly endless galleries of European paintings bring half-forgotten college art-history courses to life. You can visit just-opened special exhibits or simply stop by when you feel a need for civilization, reflected in such spaces as the Mary and Michael Jaharis Gallery. In this architecturally striking centerpiece of the Greek galleries, everything fits together in a soothing yet powerful way, from the haunting statues to the skylit barrel-vaulted ceiling of the display space. The museum's paintings and statues may be considered the mainstay of the collection, but on any given visit you can also discover or rediscover German ceramics or furniture from English country houses and French palaces. The American Wing, with its display of Tiffany and other stained glass windows, its fountain, and its wonderfully airy, parklike feeling, is another treat; the wing also has, amazingly, twenty-five period rooms, some dark and cozy, some more sophisticated (such as the Frank Lloyd Wright room). Many people love the Egyptian galleries; the crowd-pleasing Temple of Dendur in the Arthur M. Sackler Wing is another dramatic attraction in a wide-open space.

The museum offers many special events, including musical ones; they are a nice way to punctuate or end a day at the museum and are often worth a special trip. Some take place in the Grace Rainey Rogers Auditorium, but there's something especially pleasing about listening to eighteenth-century flute duets, for example, in the Temple of Dendur. Guided tours, free with museum admission, are offered daily in a variety of languages. Some tours provide an overview of the collections, others focus on specific areas such as the American period rooms, and all are good introductions to this extraordinary resource.

Of course the museum can be very crowded at times, not just on weekends but even on weekdays, particularly at special exhibits. I considered myself lucky to wait only about 45 minutes on a weekday morning to see the 2001 exhibit of "Jacqueline Kennedy: The White House Years"; the line wound through one of the nineteenth-century European painting galleries. Usually, though, weekdays are a good choice if your schedule permits, but note that the Met, like many other museums, is closed on Mondays. Keep in mind, too, that baby strollers are not permitted on Sunday, a definite drawback if you have small children and something of a plus if you don't. The museum has an active education program and is a classic destination for school trips. There is a lot here that children of almost any age can enjoy and appreciate, so making the museum family-friendly is just a matter of timing and choice of galleries. The same is true for adult visitors. Just don't try to see everything at once.

The museum has a cafeteria, a restaurant, two cafés, and two bars (one open only on weekends). Given the great variety of restaurants in the neighborhood, though, it may be more fun to eat before or after your visit.

Some of the Metropolitan Museum's neighbors along Museum Mile provide equally dazzling if more focused experiences. The **Frick Collection** (1 East 70th Street, 212-288-0700; www.frick.org) is one of these, both for its peaceful interior and its selective collection. Like the Met, it occupies an exceptional building, in this case the former home of Henry Clay Frick, the steel magnate whose collection makes up the core of the museum's exhibits. Vermeer, Rembrandt, Titian, Constable, Fragonard, and Corot are only a few of the artists whose works are on display, along with works of sculpture, French eighteenth-century furniture and porcelains, and other elegant pieces of art. It's definitely not a mass-market, dash-in, dash-out sort of place; in fact, because there are few protective barriers around the items on display, children under ten are not admitted, and the museum's brochure even suggests visiting the rooms in a specific order. It is, however, a beautiful, gracious place filled with treasures of Western world, and a lovely place to visit. I find the skylit Garden Court, with its fountain and spacious proportions, especially delightful, but, in fact, every room is special. I think of the Frick as being cool and restful in summer, warm and welcoming in winter— a museumgoer's museum, and a very manageable day-trip destination.

The **Whitney Museum of American Art** (945 Madison Avenue at 75th Street, 800-WHITNEY/944-8639; www.whitney.org) despite its emphasis on twentieth-century American art, always seems like a very traditional museum to me; I remember going to an Edward Hopper exhibit one summer Sunday a few years ago and being impressed by the number of women dressed in skirts and pumps and men in blazers. The Whitney, no doubt subliminally, seems to encourage visitors to revert to a degree of formality and adult style. Maybe it's the result of being on Madison Avenue in the absolute heart of the expensive boutique belt. The permanent collections display a variety of American art from the past century or so; the special exhibits, like the Hopper show, go into more depth, focusing on a specific artist or theme.

The museum, founded in 1930, occupies a landmark building designed by Marcel Breuer in 1966, so in a sense it's an exhibit in itself. (There is also a midtown branch at 120 Park Avenue at 42nd Street.) One particularly nice thing about the Whitney is **Sarabeth's Restaurant**. Like the other Sarabeth's, it's a particularly good place for lunch or brunch, with its emphasis on baked goods, jams, salads, sandwiches, and omelets.

You can't miss the **Solomon R. Guggenheim Museum** (Fifth Avenue at 89th Street, 212-423-3500; www.guggenheim.org). It does, after all, look a bit like a cross between a parking ramp and a flying saucer. Designed by Frank Lloyd Wright, it was completed in 1959. The circular structure, larger at the top than at the bottom, is officially described as an inverted ziggurat. You start at the top, reached by elevator, and work your way down. The main central galleries do slope a bit, since they are essentially a spiral ramp, but the side galleries are level.

The exhibits are not necessarily as unusual as the museum's building. The permanent collection is made up in large part of the Thannhauser Collection, which features works by European masters of the late nineteenth and early twentieth centuries. You may well find yourself admiring colorful and familiar works by artists such as by Cézanne, Van Gogh, Dégas, Picasso, and the only slightly less well known Camille Pisarro, whose French landscapes and street scenes may inspire you to head for the nearest Air France ticket counter. A Norman Rockwell special exhibit, at the museum from late 2001 through early 2002, was extremely popular; there's probably nothing the most scholarly art historian can write to make them hard for the general public, including children, to understand or enjoy.

Unlike most of its neighbors, the Guggenheim Museum is open Mondays, but it is closed on Thursdays. Admission is a bit higher than the norm: $15 for adults, $12 for students and senior citizens; children under twelve are admit-

The Guggenheim Museum

ted free. The Guggenheim Café is one of the more upscale and pleasant museum eating places; it serves afternoon tea as well as regular meals, and you get to enjoy your food in a setting designed by Frank Lloyd Wright.

A short walk uptown from the Guggenheim, the **Cooper-Hewitt National Design Museum—Smithsonian Institution** (2 East 91st Street, 212-849-8400; www.si.edu/ndm) presents a very different face to the world. Housed in the brick-and-limestone château-style mansion built for super-industrialist Andrew Carnegie at the start of the twentieth century, this museum focuses on decorative arts. Its large collection includes drawings, textiles, and furniture, and special exhibitions focusing on everything from wallpaper to jewelry to lighting. Unlike the various Smithsonian Institution "national museums" in Washington, D.C., the Cooper-Hewitt requires exhibit visitors to pay an admission fee: $8 for adults, $5 for students and senior citizens. Children under twelve are admitted free, but this isn't the first museum that comes to mind for families; it's more the kind of place you dip into when an especially appealing exhibit is open.

The **Jewish Museum** (1109 Fifth Avenue, 212-423-3200; www.jewishmuseum.org) is housed in the former Felix and Frieda S. Warburg mansion, built in the first decade of the twentieth century. The museum houses a major collection of Judaica, and its exhibits range from silver ceremonial objects to twentieth-century photography. "Culture and Continuity: The Jewish Journey" is a large permanent exhibit that occupies the two upper floors; rotating special exhibits are shown on the lower floors. A long-ago exhibit of Roman Vishniak's photographs of vibrant pre–World War II Polish Jewish communities was especially memorable. Two intriguing recent exhibits were "Marc Chagall: Early Works from Russian Collections" and "Berlin Metropolis: Jews and the New Century, 1890–1914." The special exhibits are usually of interest to the world at large, not just to people familiar with Jewish history and culture—though I think the extensive permanent exhibit also is of general interest, because it is so comprehensive and varied, with its displays of both objects and historical texts. It provides an informative view of 4,000 years of history and culture, with separate sections focusing on identity, tradition, the present, and the future.

Note that the museum is open Sunday through Friday and closed Saturday; it closes at 3 PM Fridays and has longer hours the other days, closing at 5:45 PM Sunday through Wednesday and at 8 PM on Thursday. The museum's Café Weissman serves an assortment of kosher food, including salads, pasta dishes, and desserts.

In 2001, a new museum opened on Fifth Avenue. The **Neue Galerie New York Museum for German and Austrian Art** (1048 Fifth Avenue at 86th Street, 212-628-6200; www.neuegalerie.org) is housed in a 1914 Beaux Arts mansion that was once the home of Mrs. Cornelius Vanderbilt III and later served as the home of the YIVO Institute for Jewish Research. The building's history and architecture are intriguingly juxtaposed with the new museum's subject. The second-floor galleries focus on Viennese art of the early twentieth century, including works by Gustav Klimt and Egon Schiele. The third floor features German art of the early twentieth century, including not only painters such as Paul Klee and Vasily Kandinsky, but also applied arts and the Bauhaus. A visit to Marcel Breuer's Whitney Museum combined with a visit to the third floor of the Neue Galerie will give you added insight into the architectural style and philosophy of Breuer, Ludwig Mies van der Rohe, and others. The Neue Galerie New York originated as a joint project of philanthropist Ronald S. Lauder and the late art dealer Serge Sabarksy. Admission is $10 for adults and $7 for students and senior citizens; children under twelve are not admitted. The museum is open to the public Friday through Monday.

The museum's café, which has gotten enthusiastic reviews, is called the Café Sabarsky after Serge Sabarsky. It serves Viennese specialties and traditional Austrian dishes, with an emphasis on pastry, and is set up to look like a Viennese café. The Café Sabarsky's hours are more extensive than those of the museum itself; the café is open from 8 AM to 7 PM Wednesday through Saturday and on Mondays, and from 1 PM to 6 PM on Sundays.

Museum shops, often footnotes to museum visits in the past, have become attractions in their own right. Beyond the traditional offerings of prints, posters, postcards, books, educational toys, and jewelry, many museum shops branch out into stationery and calendars, scarves and other textiles, and almost anything else than can be tied to museum exhibits by time, place, or mood. The shop at the Jewish Museum, for example, is a great source for menorahs and other ceremonial objects; it also has a tempting selection of klezmer and other music tapes and CDs. The engagement calendars produced for the Metropolitan Museum of Art have been popular for years; they are beautifully illustrated with items from the museum's collections and are well-designed, with ample writing space for each day of the week. Large institutions like the Metropolitan have multiple shops under one roof, with items also available directly from the museum store on the Web.

Madison Avenue, a short block to the east, has a concentration of private galleries interspersed with its famous and elegant boutiques, chocolate shops, and occasional coffee shops. Galleries dot the side streets, too, mostly on the block between Fifth and Madison. Undeniably, the purpose of the gallery exhibits is to sell paintings, prints, and other works of art, but they are usually open to the nonpurchasing public. Check newspaper and weekly-magazine listings for specifics, and you are almost sure to find a show that piques your interest.

A Saturday stroll combined with a visit to a gallery or two, followed by lunch at any one of dozens of local food spots, can feel very relaxing or glamorous. **E.A.T.** (1064 Madison Avenue, between 80th and 81st Streets, 212-772-0022), for example, is one of those places where you can get delicious sandwiches on good bread and delicious desserts for the price of a more complicated meal in the suburbs. The ambience is part of the appeal, and the food is arguably worth the price. E.A.T. is open daily from 7 AM to 10 PM, so you can also go for a late lunch or early dinner, or come in for breakfast, then find something to do until the galleries or Fifth Avenue museums open. Of course, the Upper East Side is also a hotbed of more elaborate restaurants, for which you need to make reservations. Whatever level of formality you choose, a Museum Mile meal isn't a bad way to cap a day of city pleasures.

11

More Museums, and Their Neighborhoods

Although many of New York's great museums are concentrated within walking distance of each other along Fifth Avenue or Madison Avenue, Museum Mile is by no means the end of the story. Two notable outliers are the Cloisters (which is, in fact, part of the Metropolitan Museum of Art), for its picturesque setting and medieval subject matter, and the Morgan Library, for its urbane location in Murray Hill and its manageable size. And even with the Museum of Modern Art's building closed for major renovation until 2005 and much of the museum's collection on display at P.S. 87 in Queens (see chapter 18), West 53rd Street remains a cultural destination, thanks to the new American Folk Art Museum building.

The Cloisters

When I lived in Manhattan, I used to love to take buses to places other people reach by subway. The ride on the M4 bus up Madison Avenue, west across Cathedral Parkway (110th Street), and then up, up, and farther up on Broadway fascinated me. Then and now, the bus goes from neighborhood to neighborhood, past the elegant boutiques of Madison Avenue in the Sixties and Seventies, the varied residential buildings along the northern edge of Central Park, and then into the diverse and lively world of upper Broadway. It's a long bus ride from

Midtown or below to the Cloisters, tucked away in Fort Tryon Park near the northern tip of Manhattan on a bluff overlooking the Hudson River. Here, the streets have unfamiliar names, like Fort Washington Avenue and Bennett Avenue and Pinehurst Avenue.

There's a reason people take subways. They are much faster than buses. But if you feel like seeing New York, its people and its fabric of life, it's worth the time to take this particular bus ride. And when you get there, the Cloisters is everything it should be, peaceful and dazzling in the richness of the medieval collection. The view over the Hudson is beautiful; the stone rooms, brought from European churches and monasteries, have the right dim light, the right ambience of very old stone walls, and even if ecclesiastical art isn't your favorite thing the Cloisters is the kind of place you should visit once in a while, whether to admire the art or immerse yourself in the peace of the place.

The Cloisters (Fort Tryon Park, 212-923-3700; www. metmuseum.org) is more than the place where the Metropolitan Museum of Art displays many of its medieval paintings, sculptures, tapestries, and other relics of the Middle Ages. Cloisters are the covered passages that surround the open courtyards of monasteries and other medieval structures; New York's Cloisters includes parts from several medieval French and Spanish cloisters. The gardens planted in some of the reconstructed cloisters reflect the horticultural methods of the era and add to the museum's magical quality. On display inside the building are about 5,000 works of art, primarily from the twelfth through fifteenth centuries. (Amazingly, there are thousands more works of medieval art on display at the Metropolitan Museum of Art on Fifth Avenue.)

One of the delightful parts of a visit to the Cloisters is the chance to stand in the midst of a medieval garden on a warm day and look out over the Hudson. Another pleasure is standing in a dim, stone-walled room that feels almost like the church it came from, gazing at reclining stone knights or peering through a stained-glass window. One of the most famous exhibits at the Cloisters is the series of Unicorn Tapestries, familiar from countless postcards and art-history classes. To preserve their colors and fabric, these fifteenth- and sixteenth-century masterpieces are on display in a dimly lit room, but the longer you stand there the clearer they become; the white unicorn is especially luminous in the midst of the dark greenery that surrounds it. Smaller and less colorful but no less spectacular are the extraordinarily detailed and idiosyncratic German wood faces and figures on display in other parts of the Cloisters. They catch your eye as you walk past them, and you may find yourself gazing at them for some time.

The Cloisters is open Tuesday through Sunday and does not have evening hours. There is a suggested $10 admission fee. You can reach it easily by car from the George Washington Bridge and the Henry Hudson Parkway, and parking is available; it's also within walking distance from the 190th Street stop of the A train.

Fort Tryon Park itself is pretty spectacular, thanks to its hilltop setting. During the Revolutionary War, there was a fort here named for William Tryon, the last British governor of New York. There were several estates in the area in the nineteenth century; John D. Rockefeller Jr. bought one of them in 1917. In 1927, he hired Frederick Law Olmsted Jr., whose father had designed Central Park, to turn the land into a park, which he donated to the city in 1931. The Cloisters opened in 1938 as the park's star attraction.

I remember visiting the **Dyckman Farmhouse Museum** (4881 Broadway at 204th Street, 212-304-9422; www.dyckman.org), more familiarly called the Dyckman House, with my fourth-grade class, the year we learned about New York City history and sat in rows named after the city's five boroughs. To a group of city-dwelling nine-years-olds who all lived in apartments, the Dyckman House seemed intriguingly rural, a believable vestige of a farmhouse. When the house was built in the 1780s, it certainly was remote; it truly was a farmhouse, wooded, hilly miles from the settlements at the southern tip of Manhattan, and in the midst of fields and orchards. The Dyckman family lived in the house until the 1850s. They had farmed the surrounding land since the 1600s but left during the British occupation of Manhattan (1776–83); the house that now stands on far upper Broadway is the one that was built when the family returned to Manhattan after the Revolutionary War. Broadway was already a busy road by eighteenth- and early-nine-teenth-century standards, and the house served as a place for trav-elers to stay on their way to or from the city. The farm was also hospitable to cattle on their way to market in lower Manhattan; they grazed in the fields, for a fee. During the nineteenth century, the family moved to a home elsewhere on their property and in 1870 sold their original farmhouse, which was briefly used as a hotel.

As the world grew up around it, the house deteriorated and was in poor condition by the early twentieth century. The Interborough Rapid Transit (IRT) subway line opened in 1904 and ran through upper Manhattan to reach the Bronx, leading to rising real estate prices. When developers wanted to buy the house and neighboring land, two descendants of the Dyckman family, Mary Alice Dyckman Dean and Fannie Fredericka Dyckman Welch, bought the property and gave it to the city in 1916; the Dyckman Institute donated an adjacent piece of land to the city in 1943.

The Dyckman Farmhouse Museum, opened to the public in 1916, was designated a New York City Landmark on July 12, 1967. It is operated by the City of New York Department of Parks and Recreation and the Historic House Trust. The house is open Tuesday through Saturday from 11 AM to 4 PM, and admission is free. Like the Cloisters, it's accessible via the A train, this time the 207th Street station.

The Dyckman House is Manhattan's only surviving Dutch farmhouse and remains popular with school groups as well as recreational visitors. The brick, stone, and wood exterior is in a sense the prototype for every charming Dutch Colonial house in the suburbs. The interior is furnished with English and early American pieces, including a Dyckman family cradle, and it displays some Revolutionary War relics, as well.

The Morgan Library

The Morgan Library (29 East 36th Street, 212-685-0610; www.morganlibrary.org) is a library with a difference. It began as the private library of Pierpont Morgan, a financier who became a collector. The elegant Renaissance-style palazzo that houses the collection was built for Morgan in the early 1900s next door to his home, which was on Madison Avenue at 36th Street. In 1924, Pierpont Morgan's son turned the library into a cultural institution with access for the public as well as scholars. It houses manuscripts and books so famous it's hard to believe you are actually seeing them. There is a Gutenberg Bible, circa 1455, an autograph manuscript of Mozart's Symphony No. 35 in D Major, K. 385 (the Haffner), Henry David Thoreau's Walden journal. The Library has the country's largest collection of

Rembrandt etchings, the world's largest collection of Gilbert & Sullivan scores, medieval manuscripts, more than 10,000 prints and drawings by artists from Dürer to Pollock, rare books, a tremendous variety of autographed manuscripts, and much more. Letters written to family and friends by figures such as Thomas Jefferson and Jane Austen bring history to life in a startling way; the idea of being able to read words penned by men and women whose ideas and words have become part of our lives is amazing, at least to me. Some of the items were purchased by Pierpont Morgan, while others were later added by gift or purchases.

The Morgan is a pleasure to visit. It is peaceful and luxurious, and the rooms of the original library are a vivid illustration of the sumptuous quality of life that went along with the formation of Pierpont Morgan's collection. It's a spacious place, too: a pleasant annex dating to 1928 is connected to the original library by a garden court, and a more recent addition accommodates both exhibits and public programs such as concerts and lectures.

The Morgan Library is open Tuesday through Sunday. The suggested admission fee is $8 for adults, $6 for students and senior citizens. The Morgan Court Café in the garden court is a very pleasant setting in which to enjoy lunch or other refreshment.

Murray Hill is a civilized, largely residential enclave that lends itself to walking and renewing an appreciation of New York City life. It extends from 34th Street to 40th Street between Third and Madison Avenues, and it includes a noticeable hill, which is a main part of its charm. There are some pretty brownstones and picturesque carriage houses on the side streets and some quietly elegant apartment buildings on the avenues. The ten brick carriage houses that make up Sniffen Court, off East 36th Street between Lexington and Third Avenues, are quaint and subtly glamorous enough to make any suburban visitor long to live in Manhattan. The neighborhood merges into midtown at its northern and western edges, but the East 30s have a cozy quality that's all the more appealing because the neighborhood is so perilously close to the clutter and congestion of midtown.

Just south of Murray Hill, mostly along Lexington Avenue, there's a concentration of Indian restaurants, so if you'd like to venture beyond the Morgan Court Café, the options are far-reaching. **Turkish Kitchen** (386 Third Avenue, between 27th and 28th Streets, 212-679-1810) is another interesting option, for both its reasonable prices and its tempting food.

The Museum of Modern Art

The **Museum of Modern Art** (permanent address, 11 West 53rd Street; exhibits at 45-20 33rd Street, Queens, during anticipated renovation period, 2002–2005; 212-708-9400; www.moma.org), familiarly known as MoMA, is a leading repository and display space for twentieth-century art—not just paintings and sculpture but photography, movies, and even (very notably) film stills. "Modern" is a relative term: the collection starts with works by artists like Van Gogh (considered to have a modern sensibility, particularly at the time the museum was founded in 1929) and continues on through Picasso and more recent figures. MoMa has frequent showings of all sorts of films, including early classics and modern independents.

When the museum closed its Manhattan exhibition space in 2002 for a major renovation and expansion, it scheduled a range of exhibits for MoMA QNS, as its Queens location is called; the famous building on West 53rd Street should be more impressive than ever when it reopens. According to plans, one of the museum's most appealing features, the Abby Aldrich Rockefeller Sculpture Garden, will be back, with redesigned space around it opening to the museum and making a lovely space lovelier. (Some pieces from the sculpture garden will be displayed at the New York Botanical Garden in the Bronx through the summer of 2003.)

Not far from MoMA's permanent home, there is a very child-friendly museum nearby: the **Museum of Television and Radio** (25 West 52nd Street, 212-621-6800; www.mtr.org). Essentially, you go there to watch old television shows and relive the glory days of radio. On Saturdays and Sundays, the museum has special programs for children and on Saturday mornings it has radio workshops for families. Daily screening and radio presentations take place in two theaters and two additional screening rooms. You can get a schedule of the day's programming in the museum's lobby. The Ralph Guild Radio Listening Room offers five preprogrammed listening series so you can sample the radio collection. You can also search the museum's data base for a specific radio or television program, reserve it, and go to a console room to watch or listen to it. The museum also has galleries displaying materials that relate to the history of broadcasting, and tours are available. There are frequent special events such as seminars and broadcasts, too. The museum is open Tuesday through Sunday from noon to 6 PM (8 PM on Thursday).

Not long before MoMA closed for its construction spree, the **American Folk Art Museum** (45 West 53rd Street, 212-265-1040; www.folkartmuseum.org) opened just down the street. The museum itself, formerly located near Lincoln Center, where it was known as the Museum of American Folk Art, isn't new, but its building is. The new 53rd Street building has a lot more exhibit space and a higher profile. Its collection of more than 4,000 artworks includes everything from quilts and weathervanes to paintings, dolls, and shop signs. The new museum building is open Tuesday through Sunday; admission is $9 for adults, $5 for senior citizens and students. The museum's former quarters are now known as the **Eva and Morris Feld Gallery** (2 Lincoln Square) of the American Folk Art Museum. The Feld Gallery is open daily and admission is free.

If you find yourself in the West 53rd Street museum corridor and getting hungry, there are any number of options; you are in the midst of bustling midtown Manhattan, after all. One inexpensive and low-key option, a very tempting one for anyone who likes Chinese dumplings, is **Hwa Teng** (3 West 46th Street, 212-869-4448), which specializes in Hunan cuisine. It is open daily for lunch and dinner, and the Hakow, four to an order, are especially good. The north-south blocks between 53rd and 46th Street are very short, so this is more convenient than you might think.

12

Upper Fifth Avenue:
Not Just Hospitals

For as long as I can remember, the **Museum of the City of New York** (1220 Fifth Avenue at 103rd Street, 212-534-1672; www.mcny.org) has been a quiet and fascinating spot near the relatively unexplored northeastern edge of Central Park, beyond the conventional borders of the Upper East Side. The street signs on this part of Fifth Avenue still say "Museum Mile," but the sidewalks lack the bustle of the blocks around the Metropolitan Museum of Art twenty blocks south. Nearby, various pavilions of Mt. Sinai Hospital line the east side of Fifth Avenue, and on a weekend, parking meters stand temptingly available on the west side of the avenue for people who wish to drive to the museum and its northern neighbor, El Museo del Barrio.

I don't remember when I first visited the Museum of the City of New York. It may have been on a class trip from P.S. 40, the elementary school on East 19th Street that I attended in the 1950s. Or perhaps my parents took me on a quiet weekend afternoon. What I do remember is that I loved everything about it, from the dioramas of American Indian and early colonial settlement to the toys and dollhouses on a quiet and secluded upper floor. I didn't see the dioramas on my most recent visit, and the cozy third-floor toy gallery I remember from my own childhood is now "New York Toy Stories," recently refurbished but still cozy. The museum is still full of New York history and culture, and the comfortable ambience is much the same, despite the brighter, more open feeling of the first floor. At the museum, though special exhibits come and go, the toys, period rooms, and vividly evocative paintings of New York at various stages of its development remain. It's a wonderful museum for school-age children, as well as history-minded adults.

On a more recent trip to the museum, the star temporary exhibit was "Hirschfeld's New York," on display in an unusually spacious, well-lit gallery. Al Hirschfeld, whose drawings in the *New York Times* Arts & Leisure section have been intriguing readers for decades both for their cleverness and their hidden Ninas, started his career well before World War II. The exhibit featured not just his familiar *Times* drawings but also earlier works, such as an illustration for an article about subway employees that was published in the *New York Times* magazine in 1940. It was darker and more detailed than the lighthearted drawings more recently associated with him. Overall, the exhibit was larger, more varied, and more interesting than I had expected; there were only a few other people there and it was easy to stand in front of a drawing, reading the informative label and enjoying the details. This exhibit was a good example of how the museum's mission goes beyond what is most traditional and officially "historic."

There was a time when the dollhouses were my favorite part of the museum, since they far surpassed the modest dollhouse that I owned. They are still impressive. Among the best-known are the Stettheimer dollhouse, a large structure from the 1920s, complete with a miniature art gallery of its own; several dollhouses from the early nineteenth century are on display as well. The gallery leading into the dollhouse room displays board games, ball games, and a section of other play things, many of which—like the wooden paddle with a small orange-red ball attached to it with a stretchy elastic band—may be familiar to some visitors. In addition to the toy collection on display, the museum owns thousands of toys and amusements, including puzzles, soldiers, trains, paper dolls, and several hundred children's books. Many of the items on display have special New York interest, such as New York City dolls, board games with city themes, and a model of Eloise's room in the Plaza Hotel, from the Kay Thompson book.

On the second floor, the Period Alcoves are quiet and beautiful, like life-size dioramas. They represent rooms from centuries of New York life, and the items in every tableau, from the paneling to the lighting to the ceramics and furniture, are carefully documented and described. I especially enjoyed the colonial room that includes paneling from a home on Cherry Street, a street whose identity has changed dramatically over the centuries. Cherry Street was once a place of elegant townhouses; in fact, George Washington lived on Cherry Street for several months at the start of his presidency. The first store in the chain that became Brooks Brothers was established on Cherry Street in 1818. By the middle of the nineteenth century the street had become known, among other things, for prostitution, poverty, and tenements.

To reach the alcove gallery you walk through a gallery hung with wonderfully evocative paintings of New York at various stages of its life. Like the Period Alcoves, this permanent exhibit, "Painting the Town: Cityscapes of New York," was empty of other visitors when I was there, which made each picture even more evocative. The exhibit rarely gets crowded enough to break into the mood of time travel that the displays establish so vividly.

A newer exhibit, "Broadway," presents a history of American theater. The permanent part of this exhibit is smaller than I had expected from the descriptions, but the array of old posters, pictures, and artifacts, including costumes, is well worth a visit.

There were plans for the museum to move to the beautiful Tweed Courthouse near City Hall in 2004, but the move was unlikely in mid-2002, when this book went to press. One of the nice things about its present location, in fact, is the slightly off-the-beaten track nature of upper Fifth Avenue. And although the museum is fascinating, it is of a manageable size; you can explore it thoroughly and still be ready for a walk, or lunch, or a combination of other city activities—even a visit to another museum.

El Museo del Barrio (1230 Fifth Avenue at 104th Street, 212-831-7272; www.elmuseo.org), one block up Fifth Avenue from the Museum of the City of New York, is smaller but also intriguing. Its focus is Caribbean and Latin American art, and its varied collection includes about 360 carved wooden folk-art figures (*santos de palo*), primarily but not exclusively from Puerto Rico, and approximately 2,000 pre-Columbian artifacts. "Taíno: Ancient Voyagers of the Caribbean" is an especially interesting permanent exhibit that illustrates diverse aspects of Taíno culture through stone, ceramic, and shell objects. The museum owns about 3,000 works on paper, including an extensive collection of Puerto Rican prints and posters. El Museo's 599-seat theater is brightened by murals by Willy Pogany.

When you leave the Museum of the City of New York or El Museo del Barrio, you are right across Fifth Avenue from a relatively uncrowded and natural-looking part of **Central Park.** Walking up Fifth Avenue from 96th Street, whether from the crosstown bus stop just off Fifth Avenue or after a walk west from the Lexington Avenue line's 96th Street subway station, Central Park is a surprisingly open presence on the west side of the street. The northern tip of the Jacqueline Kennedy Onassis Reservoir, ringed by a very popular jogging trail, reaches as far as 96th Street, and the East Meadow covers the low hills on the other side of the 97th Street transverse. In winter, with the leaves off the trees, the view across the East Meadow, which stretches from about 97th Street to about 100th Street, is an impressive cityscape of the Central Park West skyline.

The park's **Conservatory Garden,** between 103rd and 106th Streets, is one of the horticultural highlights of the park. This formal garden encompasses about six acres, which is a lot of ground to cover. Its wrought-iron entry gate faces 105th Street; the gate, originally from a Vanderbilt mansion, sets the tone for the garden itself. The garden is divided into three distinct sections: the Central Garden, with the Conservatory Fountain, pergolas, crab-apple allées, yew hedges, and a lawn; the North Garden, with the Untermeyer Fountain and bedding plants set to create striking floral patterns; and the South Garden, an English-style perennial garden that includes a statue representing characters from Frances Hodgson Burnett's *The Secret Garden.* The garden opens at 8 each morning and closes at dusk.

North of the garden, at the northeast corner of the park, the **Harlem Meer** is an unexpected neighborhood fishing hole, with a catch-and-release policy. It is stocked with largemouth bass, catfish, and other fish. The **Charles A. Dana Discovery Center** (212-860-1370) at the north end of the meer is an environmental education center with year-round children's workshops. Established in 1993, it is housed in a beautifully detailed Victorian-style structure that is, in fact, the newest building in the park. The Central Park Conservancy presents seasonal exhibits and events in the Great Hall at the Discovery Center, and there is a deck outside the Great Hall with a view south toward the rest of the park.

The two northernmost museums are also just a short walk from **Carnegie Hill,** a neighborhood where New York's past seems very much part of the present. Although Carnegie Hill is generally defined as the area south of 96th Street, north of 86th Street, east of Fifth Avenue, and west of

Third Avenue, to me the heart of it is somewhat north of the bustle of 86th Street, centered in the low 90s between Fifth Avenue and Lexington Avenue. There really is a hill here, and Carnegie Hill is a neighborhood of intriguing shops, beautiful brownstones and other small-scale residential buildings, made all the more appealing by its departure from the level streets typical in many other parts of Manhattan. When you walk east from Madison Avenue in the mid-90s, you can easily imagine what Manhattan must have been like before it was built up, a nicely wooded island with low hills in the middle, with slopes stretching down to the water's edge, in this case toward the East River. There are even several elegantly shuttered wood houses to heighten the feeling of having wandered into the past: two of these stand side by side at 120 and 122 East 92nd Street, and there's another, standing between two masonry townhouses, on 93rd Street between Park and Lexington Avenues.

Imagining vanished shaded hillsides and admiring elegant townhouses is only part of the fun. Upper Madison Avenue is lined with whimsical, charming, and often expensive shops, whose windows are always a treat. One that never fails to make me want to buy things I don't need and can't afford is **Dollhouse Antics** (1343 Madison Avenue at 94th Street, 212-876-2288). Through its windows you can glimpse beautiful dollhouses and all the miniature furniture you or your dollhouse-age offspring might want. (Carnegie Hill and its large- and small-scale attractions are also an easy walk from the museums farther down the Museum Mile.)

If a relaxing weekday lunch or weekend brunch is part of your agenda, **Sarabeth's** (1295 Madison Avenue, between 92nd and 93rd Streets, 212-410-7335) will fit your plans as well as it fits into the neighborhood. It's as appealing for two grownups in search of a low-key (though not low-cost) chat over omelets as it is for a family get-together. The setting and menus are festive enough for parents yet familiar enough for children; each age group can select a favorite whimsically named treat, whether it's porridge, waffles, pancakes, or Goldie lox. On my family's most recent trip to Sarabeth's, my husband enjoyed eggs Benedict, and my daughter was as impressed by the selection of jams as by her eggs/bacon/accessories special. Sarabeth's is known for preserves and a variety of delicious baked goods; its generously sized jars of preserves are available at supermarkets and specialty shops, but the novelty of eating the jam on the spot at one the several Sarabeth's restaurants in the city makes it taste even better.

13

On the Water

▪ ▪ ▪ ▪ ▪ ▪ ▪ ▪ ▪ ▪

The USS *Intrepid,* the massive cornerstone of the **Intrepid Sea-Air-Space Museum** (Pier 86, Twelfth Avenue and 46th Street, 212-245-0072; www.intrepidmuseum.org), rises majestically along Twelfth Avenue; the view evokes the days when the great passenger liners used to be visible at their piers along the Hudson. Now, the area is the site of the largest naval museum in the world, which includes not just the *Intrepid* itself, a 900-foot aircraft carrier, but also the submarine *Growler* and the destroyer *Edson.* More than thirty aircraft are displayed on the flight deck of the *Intrepid;* it is amazing to the uninitiated visitor, like me, how small many of the planes are—and how large the flight deck is. Below, the hangar deck provides another perspective on the business of aircraft carriers and the sailors and flyers who live and work aboard them.

You don't have to have a military background or be a history buff to enjoy a visit to the *Intrepid,* although many visitors do fit into that category. This is a full-service museum that provides detailed information but at the same time lets visitors go through at their own pace. There are a number of hands-on exhibits, as well as some you can actually enter—the kind children usually enjoy. But there are also fascinating photographs and artifacts that enlighten and entertain and bring life aboard ship, whether in war or peacetime, very much to life.

Open daily, the museum provides a thought-provoking and focused experience, educational, nostalgic, or exciting depending upon your age and point of view. And if a morning on the *Intrepid* has whetted your appetite for a bit of sea air and made you want to feel a deck roll beneath your feet, you might even combine your trip to the museum with a cruise around Manhattan.

Circle Line cruises (Pier 83, Twelfth Avenue at 42nd Street, 212-563-3200; www.circleline.com; cruises also leave from Pier 16, at South Street Seaport) may never have been fashionable, and they are certainly not news, but they have their own charm nonetheless. Corny, yes. Informative, also yes. You will hear stories about New York that are both familiar and perhaps apocryphal, and get wonderful views of the city. Since the trip around Manhattan Island takes about three hours, it's a substantial commitment of time, but you come away with a sense of how self-contained the island is and how important waterways and harbors are to the city's past and present. The full circuit takes you past the Statue of Liberty and Ellis Island, around the tip of Manhattan, under the Brooklyn Bridge, past Roosevelt Island, through Spuyten Duyvil, under the George Washington Bridge, and eventually back to West 42nd Street. Viewed from below, the bridges are spectacular, and it's always intriguing to get a closer view of the East River's islands. You can take the two-hour Semi Circle, offered by the same company, which goes from 42nd Street around the tip of Manhattan to the United Nations, then turns around and retraces its route. For a quick and tantalizing introduction to the Lower Manhattan skyline and close-up views of Liberty and Ellis Islands, you can also take the Circle Line's Seaport Liberty Cruise from Pier 16.

Circle Line boats sail year-round. There is at least one trip every day, and multiple trips on weekends and on warm-season weekdays. Food and beverages are available on board.

A newer company, **NY Waterway** (Pier 78, West 38th Street and Twelfth Avenue, 800-533-3779; www.nywaterway.com) also offers sightseeing cruises. It is probably best known for its commuter-ferry service from various New Jersey ports to both lower Manhattan and the West 38th Street pier, but it also offers a number of recreational possibilities. If your time is very limited, you can get a beautiful view of Manhattan and the Palisades just by riding the ferry across the Hudson River. If you'd like a more leisurely excursion, consider the 90-minute harbor cruise. Like the Circle Line, NY Waterway operates year-round, with seasonal variations in the schedule.

You can also combine a NY Waterway cruise with a visit to the *Intrepid*.

One spring-and-summer package combines admission to the *Intrepid* with a two-hour "full Manhattan" cruise, traveling north from West 38th Street (also from South Street Seaport on weekends) and including views of Grant's Tomb, the Little Red Lighthouse under the George Washington Bridge, Yankee Stadium, and more. A 90-minute cruise-and-museum package is offered year-round, leaving from the 38th Street pier, down the Hudson River, around the tip of Manhattan, up the East River to the United Nations, then turning around and pausing for several minutes at the Statue of Liberty for photographs.

NY Waterway offers some enticing tour packages that focus on the city as well as on attractions farther up the Hudson. One of the highlights of the baseball season is taking a ferry to and from a game. The company's "Yankee Clipper" and "Shea Express" ferries depart from Port Imperial (Weehawken) and Hoboken, Pier 17 at South Street Seaport, and other spots on the East Side. An especially appealing trip if you live in New Jersey is to take the train to Hoboken, then ride the ferry to the ball game.

If you already have game tickets, you can purchase tickets just for the round-trip ferry ride. Or, if you haven't yet bought tickets to a game, you can opt for a package that includes NY Waterway transportation, tickets to the game, and even a hot dog. The ferry docks are within walking distance to the stadiums.

It's also possible to get a dazzling view of the city from the water by a very familiar and traditional means: riding the Staten Island Ferry. Once, the ferry ride across New York Harbor cost a nickel. Now, it's free. Even if it cost the same as a bus or a subway, however, it would be a bargain. The ferries can be crowded—they are, after all, commuter boats for many people (including the character Melanie Griffith played in *Working Girl*)—but they can also be romantic, secluded, even nostalgic. Generations of New Yorkers and visitors have ridden them. The view as the ferry leaves Lower Manhattan is magical; the view upon your return from Staten Island is just as good. And Staten Island itself looks appealing from the water, rising, slightly hilly and partly green, out of the bay. You can also see the Statue of Liberty and the Verrazano Narrows Bridge, so all in all it's a scenic trip. To reach the ferry terminal at Whitehall Street and South Street, you can walk down from the World Financial Center through Battery Park City and into Battery Park; you can also take the N or R subway to South Ferry or the 4 or 5 subway to Bowling Green. By bus, take the M15 down Second Avenue if you are coming from the East Side, the M6 down Broadway from the West Side, or the M1 down fifth Avenue and Broadway.

The boat to the Statue of Liberty and Ellis Island is almost always very crowded, and the short ride isn't necessarily much fun. These are major expeditions around which to plan a day trip, and part of the time is simply spent waiting in line to board the boats. Still, both destinations are worth the wait.

Most people make the trip to Ellis Island and the Statue of Liberty from Battery Park. New Jerseyans, take note: You can save yourself a trip to Manhattan by boarding ferries at Liberty State Park in Jersey City as well. (There will still be lines, but at least parking is easy at Liberty State Park.) One round-trip ferry ticket includes visits to both islands. For rates and boat schedules from Battery Park, call 212-269-5755; for information about the trip from Liberty State Park, call 201-435-9499.

The Statue of Liberty and Ellis Island together make up of the **Statue of Liberty National Monument** (212-363-3200; www.nps.gov/stli). The Statue of Liberty, dedicated on October 28, 1886, and designated a National Monument on October 15, 1924, continues to be an international symbol of freedom and hope. The Statue of Liberty Museum is housed inside the statue's pedestal; the exhibits feature the history of the Statue. Ellis Island served as the processing center for millions of immigrants over a period of more than fifty years and became part of the Statue of Liberty National Monument in 1965; the island's Main Building opened in 1990 as a museum dedicated to the history of immigration. Exhibits at the three-floor Ellis Island Immigration Museum cover the history of Ellis Island and the immigration process as a whole. Among the most moving of the Ellis Island exhibits is the one called "Treasures From Home," a collection of belongings immigrants carried with them.

Ellis Island is completely wheelchair-accessible, with elevator access to all museum areas. There's a café at Ellis Island with indoor and outdoor seating. The museum exhibits in the pedestal of the Statue of Liberty are wheelchair-accessible, and there is an elevator that goes to the top of the pedestal.

Both sites were closed after the terrorist attack on September 11, 2001; Ellis Island has reopened fully, with increased security measures, but as of early June 2002 only the grounds and outdoor exhibits at Liberty Island were open to the public; tours of the grounds and exterior of the Statue were offered, but visitors were not permitted to enter the statue or the museum. Call before you plan to visit to see if the Statue has reopened.

14

Theater for All Seasons

One cool, rainy day last August, my husband and I sat at a window table at **Virgil's Real BBQ** (52 West 44th Street, 212-921-9494), watching tourists come and go in front of a large, comfortable tourist hotel. We had stopped in for lunch before a much-anticipated matinee of *The Producers.* We had gotten tickets months in advance on the enthusiastic recommendation of our daughter. What was a major and expensive overnight trip for the out-of-towners we were watching was an easy Saturday excursion for us. Theater tickets, even for hit musicals, cost less than a hotel room, and even the price of a self-indulgent meal at the popular Virgil's didn't boost the expense to hotel-room heights.

Going to the theater usually requires some advance planning. All the same, a trip to New York to see a play or musical, even a well reviewed and popular one, isn't necessarily a major logistical undertaking for anyone with a credit card and access to a listing of what's playing where.

But what about being spontaneous and thrifty? Take the train and head for the TKTS booth. The main location is at Duffy Square, a precariously angled island of sidewalk where West 47th Street meets Broadway and Seventh Avenues. Getting to it is a mini-adventure in itself. The **TKTS booth** (Duffy Square, 212-221-0013) sells tickets for 25 to 50 percent off the box-office price (plus a nominal service charge per ticket) on the day of the performance. The booth is open for evening tickets Monday through Saturday from 3 PM to 8 PM and for Wednesday and Saturday matinees from 10 AM to 2 PM. On Sundays, it's open at 11 AM for both matinee and evening tickets. Of course, TKTS may not have tickets to certain shows—but tickets for something will be available, perhaps because it has been running for years or because it doesn't have universal appeal. If it's the experience and pleasure of live entertainment you want, this can be an appealing alternative. The lines can be long, and the booth does not take credit cards, just cash and traveler's checks.

The downtown TKTS used to be at 2 World Trade Center; now it is at 186 Front Street at the corner of John Street. It is open Monday through Saturday from 11 AM to 6 PM and Sunday until 3 PM. It is certainly worth a stop if you are downtown and would like to switch gears and go to the theater. (The downtown booth sells matinee tickets the day before a performance, not the day of the performance.)

Even at half price, live New York theater is likely to cost a lot more than a night at the movies, but the event is also likely to be more memorable. Keep in mind, too, how flexible a theater-day (or night) out can be; you can bring children or leave them home, eat before, after, or not at all. The first time I took my daughter for what we might consider a girls' day out was a wintry Saturday when was she was five or six and we saw *The Secret Garden*. We had lunch beforehand at the café overlooking the Rockefeller Center skating rink, and although neither the food nor the musical turned out to be among our favorites, it was a nice way to get used to all that New York offers to families who live nearby. My husband and my son have done parallel excursions to flashier shows like *The Phantom of the Opera*, and as the children have grown up, we've expanded our list of things that all four of us enjoy.

Going to a matinee in midtown Manhattan offers the pleasant prospect of eating at one of the many reasonably priced (at least, reasonable for midtown Manhattan) restaurants that also offer a trace of big-city experience, either as tourist attractions or because the food is good. These often work not just for lunch but also for an early dinner. One good standby is **Ollie's** (200B West 44th Street between Broadway and Eighth Avenue, 212-921-5988), one of a small chain of quick-serve Chinese restaurants that serves good dumplings and, usually, good soup. Because it is fast, large, and a short walk to many theaters, it's an especially good place for lunch before a matinee. You can expect to spend about half an hour there, rarely more, and therefore don't have to worry about rushing through a luxurious meal that would be better enjoyed at a leisurely pace. Almost as fast, and also good with or without children is **John's Pizzeria** (260 West 44th Street between Broadway and Eighth Avenue, 212-391-7560), though it's not quite as much fun as the original, less spacious John's Pizzeria on Bleecker Street.

One of the small extra pleasures of seeing a production at some Broadway theaters is the chance to spend time in buildings that have so much history. The theater district has been around for a long time, and many of the theaters have names that reflect various eras—the Eugene O'Neill, the Shubert, the Helen Hayes, the Gershwin, and many more. The Winter Garden Theater (1634–1636 Broadway, between 50th and 51st Streets) may be best known for having been the site of thousands of performances of the long-running musical *Cats*. But when my family and I saw *Mamma Mia* at the Winter Garden in early 2002—somehow, we missed *Cats* during its eighteen years there—I was impressed by what an elegant and rather old-fashioned theater it was. It turns out that this theater was once the American Horse Exchange, built in the early 1880s, rebuilt after a fire in 1897, and remodeled as a theater about ten years into the twentieth century.

Sometimes the copy of *Playbill* that's distributed at the beginning of a performance provides a brief history of the theater, listing all the plays that have appeared there and adding to the overall atmosphere. Look at the painted ceilings, the ornate lighting fixtures, even the tiles in the ladies' rooms. For every stretch of cracked plaster or peeling paint in the stairwell leading to the balcony of a yet-to-be refreshed theater, there's a beautiful revival waiting to happen.

Whether you turn a theater trip into a family gathering, a friends' day or night out, or a romantic mini-getaway, getting there is straightforward. The theater district isn't just Broadway proper, of course. It spans a broader area than that, roughly from 42nd Street to 53rd Street and from Seventh Avenue to Ninth Avenue. It's easily reached by crosstown bus or subway shuttle from Grand Central or by walking uptown from Penn Station—a short though not especially attractive journey. (Tuck necklaces inside your collar and wear your handbag securely fastened!) Taxis are another option, for those who want to arrive at the theater in more traditional style. There's also a free shuttle bus from NY Waterway's West 38th Street pier, where the ferries from Weehawken come in—an appealing option if you are coming in from New Jersey and are in the mood for a scenic commute across the river. If you drive to the city, you will find the area is filled with parking garages.

Not Just Broadway

Everyone knows about Broadway. That's why, when you make an easy day or evening trip to the city, you are likely to be surrounded by crowds of people from everywhere. That's part of the fun. But there's much more to New York theater than Broadway: just read the listings and reviews in the *New York Times* or weekly magazines.

Off-Broadway is well established. Even Off-Off-Broadway has its own in-depth Web site, www.oobr.com, with detailed, well-written reviews and descriptions of Equity showcases and "nonunion productions of equivalent budget" all over New York. On any given day you can read about productions everywhere from the Lower East Side to the multiple refurbished sites on Theater Row on West 42nd Street to small, established theaters elsewhere in Manhattan and to relatively obscure destinations in the other boroughs. Prices are lower and theaters are smaller, but performance levels aren't necessarily equivalently reduced, so these are definitely theater adventures worth considering.

Off-Broadway is more institutionalized. There are dozens of Off-Broadway theaters; some of the theaters that are officially Off-Broadway offer productions as widely heralded as those on Broadway. Such familiar names as Symphony Space, the Joseph Papp Public Theater, the Cherry Lane Theater, and the Minetta Lane Theater are well publicized, sometimes well funded, and often fairly mainstream in their offerings. And they are just a sampling of the cultural bounty. Ticket prices may be marginally lower than for Broadway plays (and noticeably lower than for high-priced Broadway musicals), but this is full-fledged professional New York theater, particularly at the most widely known Off-Broadway sites.

When I think of **Symphony Space** (2537 Broadway, 212-864-1414; box office 212-864-5400; www.symphonyspace.org) I think of Gilbert & Sullivan because that's what I've seen there. It's the regular site of productions by the New York Gilbert & Sullivan Players, but it's much more than that. For more than two decades, Symphony Space has presented music marathons, film series, short-story readings, dance series, a James Joyce tribute on Bloomsday (June 16), and more. An assortment of not-for-profit groups (including the New York Gilbert & Sullivan Players) also use the space. Symphony Space has an active family program, including live music, song, dance, and storytelling and a children's film series called Film Factory.

Symphony Space is on bustling Upper Broadway near 95th Street, based in what was once the Thalia Theater, one of those traditional old Manhattan movie theaters whose floors were absolutely flat, so that seats were level with each other and one often couldn't see the screen. Seating has improved, and Symphony Space has become a two-theater arts complex, featuring the Peter Jay Sharp Theater and the rebuilt Leonard Nimoy Thalia. This part of Broadway is full of people, restaurants, shops, and, admittedly, some litter. There's a new café at Symphony Space, and, within a few blocks, so many restaurants that an afternoon or evening at Symphony Space almost has to include a meal. A few blocks south and one block east, there's **Barney Greengrass** (541 Amsterdam Avenue, between 86th and 87th Streets; 212-724-4707). Even if you didn't grow up on scrambled eggs with lox, or wonder why your grandmother's beautiful fuchsia borscht was sour instead of tasting like the raspberries whose color it resembled, Barney Greengrass is a wonderful place for brunch or lunch. It isn't very large and gets crowded, but it also doesn't take very long to eat there once you've been seated. **Pampa** (768 Amsterdam Avenue, between 97th and 98th Streets, 212-865-2929) is a popular, cash-only Argentine restaurant. This part of Broadway also is known for Cuban Chinese restaurants, a combination familiar in this neighborhood. **Flor de Mayo** (2651 Broadway between 100th and 101st Streets, 212-595-2525) is a classic and very good example. Fried plantains are a special treat here. (There's also a Flor de Mayo on Amsterdam Avenue between 83rd and 84th Streets.)

Symphony Space is an easy trip from midtown Manhattan, thanks to the 96th Street stations of the West Side IRT (1, 2, 3, 9) and the Eighth Avenue (B, C) subways. It's convenient to get to from the West Side Highway as well. Street parking may be at a premium, but there are always garages.

Miles downtown and in a more traditionally picturesque setting, the **Minetta Lane Theater** (18 Minetta Lane, between Sixth Avenue and MacDougal Street, 212-239-6200) seats slightly more than 400 people in a deep, narrow configuration. Several years ago various members of my family saw *Gross Indecency*, a play about Oscar Wilde's legal troubles, at the Minetta Lane Theater and found that the experience of being in the building added to the appreciation of the play. The building, once a factory that made tin cans, was converted to a theater in 1984. Its setting on a narrow side street off bustling lower Sixth Avenue is also part of its charm. Although the theater itself seems tucked away, it's easily reached from the West Fourth Street station of the Sixth and Eighth Avenue subways (A, C, E, F, V). And of course, since the theater is in the midst of Greenwich Village, before or after the event you can walk in virtually any direction and find picturesque streets, varied restaurants, and city atmosphere. Around the corner from the theater is the **Minetta Tavern** (113 MacDougal Street, 212-475-3850), once a speakeasy and for more than 60 years a popular Italian restaurant.

Also downtown but farther east is the now legendary **Joseph Papp Public Theater/New York Shakespeare Festival** (425 Lafayette Street, 212-260-2400; www.publictheater.org). The Public Theater has been housed in the former Astor Library on Lafayette Street, an almost disconcertingly wide street that is roughly the equivalent of Third Avenue south of Astor Place. The elegant brick and sandstone building opened in the 1850s as New York's first public library, funded by John Jacob Astor. Later it served as the headquarters of the Hebrew Immigrant Aid Society. After that organization moved out in 1965, the building was renovated and converted to serve as the home for the Public Theater. Across Lafayette Street from the theater, the majestic but no longer quite pristine facade of Colonnade Row adds to the atmosphere. The Row, dominated by marble columns, consists of four Greek Revival mansions built in 1833 to serve as homes for wealthy New Yorkers. There were once nine mansions; the four that remain have gone through and recovered from various stages of neglect and now house restaurants as well as people.

At this point, it's hard to say whether the Public is more famous for being the original home of *Hair, A Chorus Line,* and *Bring in 'Da Noise, Bring in 'Da Funk* or for its famously free summer productions at the Delacorte Theater in Central Park. The Public Theater, founded by Joseph Papp in 1954, continues to produce both new plays and familiar ones. Sometimes the tickets are hard to get for shows at the Public, but if you are alert you may be able to purchase them before a given production becomes so talked-about that tickets disappear.

The summer Shakespeare Festival is a different matter. It is free, and tickets are often even harder to get. Shakespeare in the Park productions are often star-studded and exciting. Performances, including at least one Shakespeare play each summer, take place in June, July, and August. Free tickets are distributed at the Delacorte Theater at 1 PM on the day of the performance and from 1 PM to 3 PM at the Public Theater on Lafayette Street. The Delacorte Theater is in the middle of Central Park. You can reach the theater by entering the park from Fifth Avenue at 79th Street or Central Park West at 81st Street. Once you get to the theater, lines are likely to be long. Each person can get two tickets, so if a group of friends or family members want to go together, at least half of them also have to wait in line together. In short, you need a free day, lots of reading material, a good companion, or a willing friend or relative who lives in the city and has nothing to do that day.

Almost in a straight line west from the Public Theater on Lafayette Street and the Minetta Lane Theater off Sixth Avenue, the **Cherry Lane Theatre** (38 Commerce Street, 212-989-2159 and 212-989-2020; www.cherrylanetheatre.com) has been part of theater history for decades. My parents used to go there when they were in their twenties. I used to pass it almost every morning on my long, scenic walk from the Christopher Street PATH station to my office on Greene Street. It's neatly sited at the bend of Commerce Street, one of those lovely Greenwich Village streets lined with old brick buildings and tucked away from the nearby rush of traffic. The theater building dates to 1817 and served a variety of nontheatrical purposes during its first century. In 1924 the space was converted into the Cherry Lane Playhouse. Early plays by leading twentieth-century playwrights such as Edward Albee, Samuel Beckett, and Eugene Ionesco were performed there. It is now the site of the Cherry Lane Alternative, which presents new plays by emerging playwrights.

▧ ▧ ▧

For every theater and theater company mentioned here there's another—and probably more than one—not mentioned and equally glamorous, avant garde, or just plain satisfying. Theater in many neighborhoods and many price levels is among the wonders of New York. This chapter is just the opening act.

15

Winter in the City: Holiday Memories Brought to Life

The popular image of Christmas in New York has lots of basis in reality. Brightly decorated shop windows, shoppers laden with elegantly lettered shopping bags, perhaps a little snow softening the skyline, crowds of admiring visitors massed at Rockefeller Center. The economy may wilt and climate quirks may dictate shirtsleeves, but December at Rockefeller Center, with the year's tree decorated and lit, the lacy wire angels blowing trumpets across the Channel Gardens (so called because they occupy the space between La Maison Française and the British Empire Building), and skaters whirling across the ice, is one of the glories of New York's Christmas season.

Although it's been decades since I ventured more than a yard away from the railing of a skating rink, my daughter and her friends like to skate, which is how I know that **Rockefeller Center** is a great destination for a day trip that can involve more than admiring the scenery and people. After all, if no one ventured onto the ice at Rockefeller Center, what would all those people crowded around the railing on the upper level have to look at once they tired of the flags and the angels? And for every hesitant rail-holder and laughingly embarrassed fall, there's an elegant twirler or white-haired man gliding effortlessly cross the ice who is a delight to watch.

The rink is located between 49th and 50th Streets, just east of the short north-south thoroughfare known as Rockefeller Plaza, which runs between Fifth and Sixth Avenues. It's open daily from October through April. Skating periods during the expanded holiday season generally run from 8:30 AM (occasionally 8 AM) to midnight; each period lasts an hour and a half. At this writing, weekday sessions cost $13 for adults and $9 for senior citizens and children under twelve; on weekends prices rose to $15 and $10 respectively. Skate rentals cost $7 any day of the week during the holiday season. Before and after the holiday season (late October to early November and early January to April), prices are lower and the hours are shorter. Call 212-632-3975 for more information.

Just as the skating season extends well beyond the Christmas season, so do the other pleasures of the immediate Rockefeller Center neighborhood. For many people, though, the annual Christmas spectacular at **Radio City Music Hall** (1260 Sixth Avenue at 50th Street, 212-247-4777; www.radiocity.com) is the defining attraction at this majestic venue. The

Rockefeller Center

Christmas show at Radio City features the famous precision-dancing Rockettes; the 2001 show was performed more than 200 times and featured a 3-D film tour of New York City and a video montage honoring the history of the Rockettes, as well as such favorite performances as the "Parade of the Wooden Soldiers." Radio City Music Hall can accommodate an audience of 6,000, and, with its dramatic spaces and color scheme and its famous Wurlitzer organ, this huge art deco landmark is almost a show in itself. It underwent a major renovation in 1999, and hour-long tours of its impressive interior are offered daily.

Another of the permanent pleasures at Rockefeller Center is the **Teuscher** chocolate shop (620 Fifth Avenue at Rockefeller Center, 212-246-4416; www.teuscher.com). The chocolates sold at the shop are flown in regularly from Switzerland; they are lovely to look at and wonderful to eat. The shop is another reason that, no matter how many months it is until Christmas, Rockefeller Center is worth a visit. If the Teuscher shop is too crowded, you can always switch brands and go across Fifth Avenue to purchase some wonderful **Neuhaus** chocolate from Belgium at Saks.

Even for those who do not celebrate the Christmas season, it's a glorious time to visit. Holiday shop-window displays add their magic to the mood. Just across Fifth Avenue from Rockefeller Center, the windows at **Saks Fifth Avenue** (611 Fifth Avenue, between 49th and 50th Streets, 212-753-4000) offer a view into a world of luxury and imagination. A few blocks uptown, the miniature but dazzling windows of Tiffany & Co. light up the day and night. My favorite holiday windows have always been those of **Lord & Taylor** (Fifth Avenue at 38th Street, 212-391-3344), especially when the beautifully detailed animated tableaux depict an older New York.

Not everything about New York at Christmas has to do with shopping, of course, and Rockefeller Center and its immediate environs are by no means the only places to share in the festive holiday spirit. The Rockefeller Center tree may be the most famous one in New York, and in some ways the most spectacular because it is set against the quintessentially urban backdrop of the sleek gray buildings, but other decorated trees are also well worth seeing.

Each year, the **American Museum of Natural History** (West 79th Street and Central Park West, 212-769-5100; www.amnh.org) has a Christmas tree decorated with wonderfully colorful and imaginative origami creations. The museum also hosts a weekend family festival in December to help celebrate the African American cultural holiday Kwanzaa, which is observed from December 26 through January 1. In 2001, the festival included drumming and other musical performances, dance, and a fashion "safari" highlighting designers from several African nations as well as the Caribbean and the Americas.

At the **Metropolitan Museum of Art** (Fifth Avenue at 82nd Street, 212-535-7710; www.metmuseum.org) there's another dramatic and unusual tree, in this case a candlelit spruce highlighted by a Neapolitan Baroque crèche, which features elaborate, costumed eighteenth-century figures. It's on display from late November through early January, with lighting ceremonies Friday and Saturday evenings. In 2001, for the first time, the Metropolitan Museum of Art also displayed a menorah to mark Hanukkah, the Jewish Festival of Lights. The large and very decorative menorah dates to the late eighteenth century and is believed to have come from a synagogue in Eastern Europe.

Returning to the theme of chocolate, there are freestanding **Neuhaus** shops near both the Metropolitan Museum of Art (922 Madison Avenue at 74th Street, 212-861-2800) and the Museum of Natural History (2151 Broadway at 75th Street, 212-712-2112).

Although it's quite a detour from the massive museums flanking Central Park, the **Cloisters** (Fort Tryon Park, 212-923-3700), home to much of the Metropolitan Museum's collection of medieval art, is also a delightful holiday-season destination. Easily accessible by car from the Henry Hudson Parkway and by public transportation via the M4 bus, the Cloisters is seasonally decorated with berries, herbs, and greens. It hosts an especially atmospheric afternoon Christmas concert series.

Saint Patrick's Cathedral (Fifth Avenue at 50th Street), directly across Fifth Avenue from Rockefeller Center, encourages reflection as well as celebration and admiration. Whether at Christmas or any other time of year, the Cathedral is an impressive place for visitors of all faiths. This Gothic structure, designed in 1859 by James Renwick and completed in 1879, seats about 2,200. The interior is very grand and spacious, and there is a beautiful rose window on the Fifth Avenue end of the building. The cathedral is usually open to the public from 8 AM to 8:45 PM, but keep in mind that although about three million people visit the cathedral each year, this is not primarily a tourist destination but a house of worship, with frequent, regularly scheduled masses.

The front steps of Saint Patrick's are sometimes almost as bustling with tourists and people watchers as the front steps of the Metropolitan Museum; they're a quintessentially New York place. The reflection of the cathedral, especially its spires, in the shiny exterior walls of adjacent buildings is one of the quirky yet classic sights of the city; stand south and west of the cathedral to get the best perspective on this reflected view.

16

The Bronx:
Flora and Fauna

I don't love zoos, but I've come to realize that most people, young and old, do. They like to talk to the primates, admire the peacocks, stare at the giraffes, pet the farm animals. Even those of us who can take an afternoon at the zoo and then leave it with some relief can admire the **Bronx Zoo** (Bronx River Parkway and Fordham Road, 718-367-1010; www.wcs.org), however, and maybe even like it. It's a terrific zoo, not just the best in the metropolitan area, but one of the best in the nation. It is one of five New York City facilities of the Wildlife Conservation Society (WCS), formerly the New York Zoological Society.

The Bronx Zoo opened in 1899 with 22 exhibits and 843 animals. Now it occupies 265 acres and has well over 6,000 animals. Its mission was to educate the public, advance the study of zoology, and protect wildlife, and over the years it has done all that and more. Visitors can see more than 600 species, many of them in habitats remarkably close to their native habitats; the Wildlife Conservation Society also has such behind-the scenes facilities as the Wildlife Health Center, providing care to the more than 15,000 animals under the Wildlife Conservation Society aegis in New York.

For some visitors, the view of the lions on an open plain, separated from human observers by a deep trench and a surprisingly unobtrusive wall, may be among the most memorable parts of the zoo. For others, the sense of wonder comes from seeing the giraffes on a hillside grazing on impossibly high tree limbs. When the *African Plains* exhibit, home of the lions, opened in 1941, the Bronx Zoo was the first American zoo to exhibit animals in their natural habitat.

Wild Asia, which opened in 1971, is a seasonal attraction, open only from April to October. In season, it is one of the must-sees, replete with tigers, elephants, and other dramatic animals. The Bengali Express monorail ride, open May through October, takes you through Wild Asia. *Jungle World,* which opened in 1985, is a year-round indoor tropical rain forest bustling with tree kangaroos, Malaysian tapirs, and other denizens of Asian rain forests. *World of Darkness* is another indoor environment; those who like bats (and other creatures of the night) love the exhibit.

Among the exhibits, the *Congo Gorilla Forest* is perhaps the universal favorite. The last time I was there, my husband, daughter, and I loved watching the inhabitants of the Gorilla Forest interact with each other and with their audience. This 6.5-acre African rain-forest habitat is home to 400 animals, including 23 lowland gorillas, and is a thought-provoking and absorbing part of any zoo visit. What is going on behind those bright-eyed, wrinkled faces, and how much skill do those nimble hands really have?

The Children's Zoo is stellar. It has a delightful prairie-dog tunnel exhibit, an area where children can pet farm animals, and a good variety of other interactive learning experiences. I remember taking my daughter there when she was a toddler, accompanied by her brother, who was then about ten, and one of his friends, the same age. Despite the gap in ages, all three children had a wonderful time, even though my daughter has insisted for years that the boys pushed her down a hollow tree trunk that was part of one of the exhibits.

Something that children will especially enjoy but will be a delight for adults as well is the zoo's annual Holiday Lights show, which runs from mid-November to January 1. It is what it sounds like: lots of lights, on trees, buildings, and, perhaps best of all, on 140 animal sculptures, some of them animated. During this festival, some popular exhibits are open, including the Monkey House and the Children's Zoo.

The obvious way to get to the Bronx Zoo, especially with small children and a stroller or two, is by car. There are two parking lots on site, and the walk from the eastern parking lot to the main attractions takes you past grazing bison, among other sights, before you reach a grand architectural set of broad steps. The zoo exit off the Bronx River Parkway is well marked. Metro-North (to Fordham Station) and the 2 or 5 subway lines will also get you there, as will a Liberty Line (718-652-8400) express bus from Manhattan.

During a morning or afternoon visit to the zoo, you will do a lot of walking, watching, listening, and wondering. You will probably get hungry or thirsty, as well as tired; there are several places to eat, and many people bring their own food and picnic, as well. The zoo's Terrace Cafe is open year-round; in addition to snack stands throughout the zoo, there are seasonal food stands at Asia Plaza and African Market. The zoo is open every day of the year; an admission fee is required every day but Wednesday, and there are additional fees for certain rides and areas, such as the Congo Gorilla Forest, Bengali Express Monorail, Skyfari, and Children's Zoo.

The **New York Botanical Garden** (Fordham Road and Bronx River Parkway, 718-817-8700; www.nybg.org), just north of the Bronx Zoo, is to public gardens what the Bronx Zoo is to zoos—one of the leading examples of its type in the world. The highlight of this 250-acre garden is the beautiful Enid A. Haupt Conservatory, a recently restored Victorian-style glass house. Aside from the sheer loveliness of the structure itself, the series of gardens it contains are impressive. The Conservatory includes hot, humid tropical rain forests and hot, dry deserts, making it an especially delightful destination on cold winter days.

Several years ago, right around Christmas, my husband and I made the trip to the Botanical Garden to see the Holiday Train Show, which is set up in the Conservatory from late November through early January. It is an enchanting collection of models of famous New York City buildings; yes, trains run through the city, but they aren't necessarily the main event. When you think of model trains, you may think of children, and certainly lots of parents who were there that day had done exactly that. This is certainly not a place just for children, or even primarily for them: it's a train show that transcends a child's delight in model trains. It's an exhibit to linger over, to appreciate the planning and the craftsmanship of the model historic buildings, which are constructed of an amazing array of natural materials. The overall layout includes trains and trolleys traveling over nearly 1,000 feet of track in an imaginative setting of rivers, waterfalls, mountains, and bridges—including the Brooklyn Bridge—and past dozens of buildings. Among our favorites were the Flatiron Building, known for its triangular shape and re-created here with white pinecones, lotus pods, and dried beans; lemon and oak leaves are used for horizontal ornamentation. The art deco Chrysler Building is an attention-getter in real life and in the train show. Hazel branches make up the contoured areas, and honeysuckle sticks and pods make up the rest, with details provided by pods and gingko leaves. Grand Central Terminal is another of the more familiar buildings; this one has a roof made of magnolia leaves and a facade of sand and sycamore bark.

Holiday Reflections: A Festival of Light, which takes place during the same period as the train show, is another special holiday treat at the Enid A. Haupt Conservatory. There are lights in the honey locust trees that lead to the entrance and a decorated tree in the Entrance Plaza.

Among the other highlights of the New York Botanical Garden is the Peggy Rockefeller Rose Garden. Containing 2,700 plants and more than 260 varieties, this garden includes only roses available to the home gardener. Within that broad group are many modern roses, including hybrid teas, grandifloras, and floribundas, as well as old roses developed before 1867. The roses are labeled, so if you see roses that you especially like, you will know what to look for the next time you buy plants. Interestingly, the garden was designed in 1916 by Beatrix Jones Farrand, a well-known landscape architect; funding (from Peggy and David Rockefeller) and actual construction of the garden did not come until many decades later: the garden was dedicated in September 1988.

The Rock Garden is another of the Botanical Garden's treasures. It is one of the largest public rock gardens in the country, with massive rocks brought in to create the illusion of mountain scenery, complete with a waterfall, rock outcroppings, and streams. Alpine plants, dwarf conifers, woodland plants, and wildflowers are just some of the flora in the Rock Garden. Different planting areas reflect different types of soil, moisture, and exposure.

The more you explore the more you will find. There are other gardens within the Botanical Garden, as well as special events throughout the year. You can explore on your own or take advantage of the variety of tours available at the Botanical Garden. Narrated tram tours are offered year-round at twenty-minute intervals, providing an overview of the gardens and grounds. There are less-frequent narrated golf-cart tours from April to October; these require reservations. There are also walking tours several days a week.

Like the Bronx Zoo, this is a destination that calls out to be reached by car; it's off Exit 7W of the Bronx River Parkway and parking is available. There is a shuttle bus from Manhattan on Fridays and weekends April to October and on Saturdays in November and December; call 718-817-8700 for information and reservations. You can also get to the Garden via Metro-North from Grand Central Station, and if you're using the subway, the D train station at Bedford Park Boulevard is about eight blocks away.

On the other side of the Bronx, and on a smaller and more intimate scale, there's another wonderful garden. **Wave Hill** (Independence Avenue and West 249th Street, Riverdale, 718-549-3200; www.wavehill.org) is "a public garden and cultural center," according to its brochure. It is also an extraordinarily peaceful enclave in Riverdale; on the far western edge of the Bronx, Riverdale is full of lovely houses and winding tree-lined streets.

Wave Hill House itself was originally a country home, built in 1843. William Henry Appleton, a member of a family that prospered in publishing, owned it from 1866 to 1903. He enlarged and improved it and invited many prominent guests to stay there, including Thomas Henry Huxley and Charles Darwin. Theodore Roosevelt's family rented the house for two summers in the early 1870s, and Mark Twain leased it in the early 1900s. In 1903, George W. Perkins, a partner of J. P. Morgan, bought Wave Hill House to form part of a larger estate, which also incorporated the site of Glyndor House, the other elegant former country home that graces the property. Appleton had built the gardens and greenhouses. Perkins added terraces and other greenhouses, as well as recreational facilities. The famous maestro Arturo Toscanini lived at Wave Hill from 1942 to 1945 after leaving Italy during the Fascist era. In 1960, Perkins's descendants deeded the property to New York City. It is an idyllic combination of carefully tended gardens and lawns, anchored by the two elegant houses that are now used for cultural activities.

It's easy to get to Wave Hill by car from the Henry Hudson Parkway. (You can also reach it by taking a Metro-North Hudson Division train to

Riverdale or taking the 1 or 9 subway to 231st Street and transferring to a local bus—Bx7 or Bx10—for the trip west across the Bronx; another option is to take the A train to 207th Street and transfer to the Bx7 bus.) There are little green signs pointing the way to Wave Hill, both on the Parkway itself to the exit (252nd Street northbound, 254th Street southbound) and on surface roads once you have left the Parkway. When you turn west from the Parkway, then south on Independence Avenue to reach the entrance gate at 249th Street, you will find yourself in a lovely residential neighborhood with houses, lawns, and lush landscaping. On the sun-dazzled morning in early October when I visited Wave Hill, I saw a thriving apple tree, bright with big red apples. When you turn into the Wave Hill driveway, you pay the very reasonable seasonal $4 fee and discover that it includes parking; admission is free from mid-November to mid-March, as well as all day Tuesdays and on Saturday mornings the rest of the year. (Wave Hill is open Tuesday through Sunday year-round but is at its peak from mid-spring through early fall.)

Easy access and budget-friendly admission are a nice start, but when you leave the parking lot and start up the path to the Great Lawn, things get even better. The lawn is wide, and at the far end there's a wooden structure framing a view of the Hudson River and the Palisades on the other side of the river. The Pergola Overlook is a perfect sitting area, surrounded by greenery and flowers, with an amazing view that reminds you that the Hudson is one of the nation's most scenic rivers.

It's tempting to go straight to Pergola Overlook and gaze out at the river through the plantings, but once you have done that, you will want to retrace your steps and visit the gardens. The Flower Garden is, in fact, almost directly on your right when you enter Wave Hill from the parking lot. The flowers are amazing, colorful, wonderfully varied, and neatly labeled. When I was there in early October, there was a delightful array of red, yellow, orange, and purple flowers—brilliantly colored dahlias, asters, salvias, morning glories, and more. Paths, benches, trellises, and the graceful cedar fence that defines the garden's borders all work together to make this an especially pleasant place to linger.

The Conservatory and Greenhouses separate the Flower Garden from the next series of delightful outdoor gardens. On a lovely early fall day, they take something of a supporting role, but they are certainly worth a visit to admire the cacti and succulents growing on one side and the tropical plants on the other side. What I liked better, almost as much as the Flower Garden, was the Herb Garden. Like the Flower Garden, it has lots of little pathways and ample labeling for its large collection of plants used for medicinal, nutritional, ceremonial, and other purposes. In addition to standbys such as basil, the Herb Garden has a wide variety of more exotic plants, such as sugar cane, cinnamon yam, and eucalyptus. The next series of garden "rooms" features the Aquatic Garden, flanked by two long pergolas. The Aquatic Garden, like the other gardens at Wave Hill, is both small and spectacular, filled with an impressive variety of water plants, including purple and pink water lilies. Below Wave Hill House, there is yet another outdoor area to explore—the Herbert and Hyonja Abrons Woodland, with a trail winding through a ten-acre section of woodland and meadow closer to the river. Wave Hill House is connected to the main gardens by a driveway. It has a cafe, a well-stocked gift shop, and a great veranda overlooking the river. (At the time of this writing, the new Perkins Visitor Center, on the present site of the Garden Garage, was scheduled to open in 2002, with, among other things, an expanded gift shop.)

Wave Hill is a great place to go for a half-day of garden glory, especially during the week. Although there were a few children in strollers with nannies or parents the day I visited, most of the other visitors were either people just sitting and relaxing or small groups of women, seemingly from out-of-town garden clubs. Throughout the year, Wave Hill sponsors lectures and other events that are especially rewarding for visitors with a serious interest in gardening and landscape design. It offers programs in environmental education, horticulture, landscape history, visual, performing, and literary arts, and more. It's also, especially on weekends, a very family-friendly place, with festivals and projects for the entire community. For example, its October 2001 fall festival highlighted a Latin American and Caribbean-inspired Plaza de Calabaza (Gourd Place). Children had the opportunity to weigh pumpkins and lots of colorful, interestingly shaped gourds and to drink *yerba mate* from a dried gourd. There were musical instruments made of gourds on display, and a family art project focused on creating objects from dried gourds. The gardens featured a selection of pumpkins, squash, and gourds with explanations of how to grow them, and visitors were invited to taste grilled samples of the produce. The Wave Hill Cafe offered pumpkin soup, among other things. There are garden walks, concerts, and family art projects on weekends throughout the year, and for those who prefer to bring their own food, there is a picnic area just north of Glyndor House.

Wave Hill is a lovely place to walk, but it's important to note that the gravel paths may be difficult for people with limited mobility, and pushing a stroller along the paths may also be challenging. There is a courtesy cart to provide shuttle service from the front gate to Glyndor House and Wave Hill House, however.

The Bronx isn't all flowers and wildlife. Come spring, summer, and early fall, there's **Yankee Stadium** (161st Street and River Avenue, 718-293-6000) for a day or night of baseball. Of course you can drive there from virtually anywhere in the metropolitan area if you leave home early and don't mind potentially long waits at river crossings, intersections, and entrances to and exits from parking lots. You can also take the 4 subway train from Grand Central Terminal if you prefer not to drive and can coordinate your suburban train schedule back home from Grand Central with the time the game ends. You can also take the **NY Waterway Yankee Clipper ferry service** (800-533-3779; www.nywaterway.com) to and from the game. This is a delightful way to add an extra dimension to the experience, and avoid having to deal with traffic. The fun and convenience don't come cheap—the 2001 price for an adult was $69—but that includes round-trip transportation, a seat at the baseball game, and a hot dog, a soft drink, and a souvenir. When you consider parking fees, tolls, mileage, and the possibility of being stuck in traffic, the cost of the ferry service begins to seem much more reasonable. The ferry is especially convenient for New Jersey baseball fans, since it has departure points both in Hoboken and Weehawken, but it may work well for Long Islanders, too, given its several departure points on Manhattan's East Side.

Tucked away in several neighborhoods and faithfully maintained by the Bronx County Historical Society are several historic houses, almost ignored by the outside world, open on limited schedules, but interesting and sometimes haunting reminders of a Bronx, city, and time that have otherwise vanished. One of these is the **Poe Cottage** (Grand Concourse and Kingsbridge Road, 718-881-8900), the last home of Edgar Allan Poe. He lived in the cottage, in what was then known as Fordham Village, from 1846 to 1849. The cottage was moved to its present location in then newly created Poe Park in 1913 and has been open to the public as a museum and memorial since 1917. It is open Saturdays from 10 AM to 4 PM and Sundays from 1 PM to 5 PM; it is closed from mid-December to mid-January. Driving is probably the most convenient choice for people coming from outside the city, but it's also accessible from the Fordham stop of Metro-North and via subway on the D train (205th Street) and 4 train (Mosholu Parkway). The **Valentine-Varian House** (3266 Bainbridge Avenue at East 208th Street, 718-881-8900) is a lovely fieldstone house that was built in 1758 along the old Boston Post Road in the midst of what was then farmland. The Valentine family, who lived there during the Revolutionary War, had to flee the house because battles were being fought nearby. Isaac Varian later bought the house, and his family stayed there for three generations. The house is now the Museum of Bronx History. Like the Poe Cottage, the Valentine-Varian House is open Saturdays from 10 AM to 4 PM and Sundays from 1 PM to 5 PM. Before visiting either house, you should call to confirm that the site will be open.

The Poe Cottage and the Valentine-Varian House are two of the four houses in the Bronx that are part of the Historic House Trust of New York City. Another is the **Bartow-Pell Mansion Museum** (Shore Road, Pelham Bay Park, 718-885-1461), a gray stone structure dating to 1842 and set in formal gardens. The fourth is the **Van Cortlandt House** (Van Cortlandt Park, Broadway and 246th Street, 718-543-3344), a mid-eighteenth-century farmhouse filled with eighteenth- and early nineteenth-century furniture. Like the first two, they serve as refreshing reminders of what the city looked like before it was a city.

17

Brooklyn:
A City in a Borough

Brooklyn is huge. With a population of more than two million people and an area of eighty-one square miles, it is larger than most American cities. In fact, for much of the nineteenth century it was the third-largest city in the United States. Brooklyn evokes images from virtually every era and every field of endeavor. The Dodgers. Woody Allen. Barbra Streisand. Walt Whitman. Coney Island. A borough accessible from Manhattan via one beautiful bridge and two also-rans. Street-corner singers creating 1950s rock music. Ethnic diversity most other places only dream of. Brownstone neighborhoods that pioneered row-house revival, and blocks of apartment buildings that shaped visions of twentieth-century urban America. Brooklyn is a place that inspires passionate loyalty in those who have lived there. It's also a great place to visit—many times, since there's far too much to see and do in one day's visit—and it is easy to reach from the rest of the metropolitan area.

In my very early childhood, my father and I used to take the subway from our family's apartment on East 22nd Street and cross the East River to go to the dentist. Dentists' offices had not yet become the friendly, comfortable places they generally are now, and going to Brooklyn, even to an office in Brooklyn's tallest office building, the gold-topped Williamsburgh Savings Bank Building (1 Hanson Place, and now occupied by another bank), had no glamour or charm. Little did I know when I rode the subway to the Williamsburgh Savings Bank how close we were, for example, to **Peter Luger Steak House** (178 Broadway, 718-387-7400), where I finally ate for the first time in the mid-1990s; it was a summer Sunday afternoon, and my husband and I had been in Manhattan, wandering through an air-conditioned museum. We called from Manhattan and were lucky enough to reserve a table during a summer-Sunday lull in business—it was about three in the afternoon. We drove to Brooklyn, found a parking space almost directly across the street, and were seated and served without delay. The steak was as wonderful as it's supposed to be, the ice-cream sundae we shared for dessert was enormous and generously covered with whipped cream, and the service was a perfect blend of efficiency and cordiality. We have been back several times since with our children, who are equally enthusiastic. Since that first spur-of-the-moment trip, we have discovered that reservations are not always easy to come by for prime weekend hours—call well in advance. Although your meal will not be inexpensive, a trip to Peter Luger is money well spent. Credit cards are not accepted, so bring plenty of cash.

Peter Luger opened as a beer hall in the 1870s, and a lot has changed in Brooklyn since then. Whole neighborhoods of factories have been built, have thrived, and have closed; the waterfront has gone through several identities; miles of brownstones have flourished, crumbled, and in some cases revived. There are apartment buildings where there was once a baseball field, artists' studios where there were once warehouses. Williamsburg itself, in the northwestern corner of Brooklyn, has evolved into a fledgling artists' colony and lower-rent haven for people in their twenties and thirties. Although it may be unfamiliar, it is not remote: **Bedford Avenue,** the commercial main street of Williamsburg, is the first stop on the L train from the station at 14th Street and First Avenue in Manhattan. There are galleries, restaurants, and retail adventures to be discovered in Williamsburg, and Bedford Avenue is a good place to start exploring this evolving area.

The streets of **Brooklyn Heights,** across the water from the tip of Manhattan at the point where the East River turns into Upper New York Bay, are less adventurous. In fact, they're so charming that they almost don't seem like places where people might really live and work. But they are. Starting in the early nineteenth century and for decades after, Brooklyn Heights was a suburb of Manhattan; it was linked to Manhattan by subway in 1908. For a time in the twentieth century it became somewhat neglected, with many of its lovely buildings turned into rooming houses. Now it is a place of beautiful tree-lined streets, picture-book town houses, elegant brownstones, breathtaking views, and the endless commercial and culinary temptations of its main thoroughfare, Montague Street. It was listed on the National Register of Historic Places in 1965 and was the first Historic District in New York City.

The area is bounded by Court Street and Cadman Plaza on the east and Atlantic Avenue on the south. The Booklyn–Queens Expressway borders it to the north, the East River to the west. You can reach Brooklyn Heights by crossing the Brooklyn Bridge by car, or, more scenically, by bicycle and on foot, then turning toward the low-rise streets that are visible from the exit ramp. Or you can take the subway; the 2 train will take you to Clark Street, the M, N, R, 2, and 5 will take you to Court Street. Ferries were once the main mode of transportation for people commuting between Manhattan and Brooklyn, and reading a few lines of Walt Whitman's "Crossing Brooklyn Ferry" is a good way to set the mood for a few hours spent admiring the abundant relics of the nineteenth century that make up so much of Brooklyn Heights. Whitman lived in Brooklyn Heights as a child and worked near Fulton Ferry when he edited the *Brooklyn Eagle* in the 1840s.

Once you reach Brooklyn Heights, you might want to head for the **Esplanade,** a narrow park that runs along the edge of Brooklyn Heights above the waterfront and offers dramatic views of Manhattan. You have to walk through the Heights to get to the Esplanade, and even the walk along Joralemon Street from the subway station at Borough Hall, for example, is so delightful and so full of tempting detours onto small side streets—for example, Sidney Place and Garden Place—that it will probably take a while to find your way to the Esplanade. A walk along the Esplanade is one of those perfect urban experiences, with a famous skyline on one side, an intriguing mix of people all around you, and ornate brownstones forming an elegant wall between the Esplanade and Columbia Heights, the first street inland.

Columbia Heights, with its views across the Esplanade to the water and beyond to Manhattan, is built on a somewhat grander scale than many other streets in the neighborhood. Its imposing brownstones date to the middle of the nineteenth century and include the one from which Washington Roebling supervised the construction of his father's masterpiece, the Brooklyn Bridge. The streets with tree and fruit names are generally more intimate in scale. **Cranberry, Orange, Poplar,** and **Pineapple Streets** parallel each other at right angles to Columbia Heights; they are as charming as their names and are accompanied by several other less poetically named streets, notably **Middagh** and **Clark,** that are equally delightful. **Willow Street,** parallel to Columbia Heights, has a number of especially pretty brick rowhouses. Throughout the area, there are lots of Greek Revival townhouses, with just enough new construction and apartment buildings mixed in to provide variety and a sense of present-day real life. There are even a few clapboard houses to suggest a more rural moment in time. The enormous building that was once the **St. George Hotel,** built in 1885 and expanded twice after that, occupies a full block between Hicks and Henry Streets and Clark and Pineapple Streets. In the 1930s, it was a fashionable hotel, albeit one that allowed Lower East Side boys like my father to swim in its pool; by the 1970s it was shabby and sad. Now it has a variety of identities; one section serves as housing for the elderly, another as residential co-ops, another a condominium.

Lively Montague Street is almost the halfway point between the northern and southern sections of Brooklyn Heights. All sorts of businesses line the street, but it's especially notable for having an impressive number of restaurants reflecting equally impressive ethnic diversity. On just one side of the street on one block are the Happy Days Diner, Annie's Blue Moon Café, Amin Indian Restaurant, Coq Hardi (food of Provence), Mezzo (French and Italian food), French Brunch (with a New Orleans accent), and Green's Asian Restaurant on the second floor of a corner building. And at the southwest corner of that same block is the **City Market Café** (166 Montague Street at Clinton Street, 718-422-1055), which offers semi-subterranean dining and almost limitless variety. A few blocks east, the **Heights Café** (84 Montague Street at Hicks Street, 718-625-5555) is another good neighborhood spot; it has the added benefit of a good view of the street from the terrace tables. Nearby, **Teresa's** (80 Montague Street, 728-797-3996) offers pierogi and other Polish specialties.

The streets south of Montague Street are for some reason not quite as well known as the quaintly named streets at the northern edge of the Heights. Perhaps it's a matter of name: Remsen Street doesn't sound as romantic as Cranberry Street, and Joralemon looks hard to pronounce. Still, these streets are seductive and well worth exploring. Grace Court, for example, dead-ends with a great view of the water and Manhattan, and it has the added advantage of being lined by a combination of old houses, old apartment buildings, and what look like either backyards or community gardens; whichever they are, they're delightful pockets of greenery.

The **Plymouth Church of the Pilgrims** (Orange Street between Henry and Hicks Streets), built in 1850, is worth a thought as well as a second look. It was here that the Reverend Henry Ward Beecher, brother of *Uncle Tom's Cabin* author Harriet Beecher Stowe, delivered powerful anti-slavery sermons in the 1850s; he served the church, then known as Plymouth Church, until 1887. The Tiffany windows that once adorned the church are now in Hillis Hall, which is behind the church. In the Cobble Hill neighborhood, across Atlantic Avenue from Brooklyn Heights, you can see a few Tiffany windows (most were destroyed more than 60 years ago in a fire) at **Christ Church** (Clinton Street at Kane Street). This church was built in 1840 and designed by Richard Upjohn, who was known for his Gothic churches.

The **Brooklyn Historical Society** (128 Pierrepont Street, 718-222-4111; www.brooklynhistory.org) occupies an impressive, highly ornamented nineteenth-century building; at the time of this writing it was undergoing major renovation, with work expected to be completed in late 2002. The Historical Society was founded in 1863; part of its mission is to preserve objects of almost any kind that relate to Brooklyn history. Its collection includes Native American tools, seventeenth-century drawings, period furnishings, Brooklyn Dodgers memorabilia, pushcarts, West Indian carnival costumes—even a cable-carrier wheel from the Brooklyn Bridge. The Historical Society also offers educational programs, develops neighborhood history guides, and sponsors a Walks and Talks series. It's a wonderful resource for anyone who would like to know more about Brooklyn.

The **New York City Transit Museum** (718-694-5100; www.mta.nyc.ny.us/museum), which closed for renovation in 2001, was expected to reopen in 2003. Its location, in the authentic-looking but decommissioned subway station at the corner of Boerum Place and Schermerhorn Street, just east of Brooklyn Heights, inspires nostalgia. It is an easy walk about midway between two working stations: Borough Hall on the 2, 4, and 5 lines and Hoyt-Schermerhorn on the A and C trains. When my family visited the museum in the late 1990s on a rainy Sunday afternoon, we felt as though we had entered a time warp; it was hard to believe that the train doors wouldn't close soon and the trains start moving. Station renovations are expected to include fire and safety upgrades and improved climate control. There will be a new art gallery, a renovated lecture/media room, and an expanded education department. In addition to the old subway cars that will continue to be star attractions, there will be a new exhibit about surface transportation—that is, buses and trolleys, with interactive exhibits and more than 200 trolley models.

> During the renovation period, the museum is presenting exhibits at its Gallery Annex at Grand Central Terminal. Although it lacks the nostalgic charm of the old, unused subway station that is the permanent transit museum, it is an interesting destination. The Annex is off the Main Concourse in the Shuttle Passage next to the Station Master's Office. The popular **Museum Store** at Grand Central Terminal is open daily; there is also a store at the Times Square Visitors Center (1560 Broadway between 46th and 47th Streets).

Brooklyn Heights and its surrounding areas, such as Cobble Hill and Carroll Gardens, represent only a tiny sliver of all that Brooklyn has to offer. Opportunities abound for those intrigued by brownstones—their architecture and the lifestyles they've represented over the years—to wander and explore. Park Slope is perhaps the best-known of the brownstone regions, but by no means the only one; as with so much else about the borough, your travels are limited by your own time and energy, not by the extent of the offerings. One excellent way to introduce yourself to Brooklyn is to take an organized tour. Those offered by **New York Like a Native** (www.nylikeanative.com) are especially appealing, thanks in large part to the expertise and personality of the company's founder, Norman Oder. His "Brooklyn Brownstone Tour" is just one of several informative and varied walking tours the company offers.

The "Park" of Park Slope is **Prospect Park**. It bears certain resemblances to Central Park, having been designed in the nineteenth century by the same firm, Olmsted and Vaux. It encompasses more than 500 acres and is bounded on the north by Eastern Parkway, on the south by Parkside Avenue, on the east by Ocean Parkway and Washington Avenue, and on the west by (surprise!) Prospect Park West and Prospect Park Southwest.

Prospect Park is a beautiful park, and a nice change of pace from Central Park if you want to get a sense of how much a large, well-designed park means to a densely populated urban area. Prospect Park has the usual design features and amenities, such as a 60-acre lake, a 90-acre meadow—even a heavily wooded area known as the Ravine. You can skate at the Wollman Center and Rink, listen to music at the Bandshell, take your children to one of several playgrounds, rent a boat at the Boathouse, ride the Carousel. The Carousel, open April through October, makes playground merry-go-rounds look insignificant. It dates to 1912, and the carved wooden animals include not just horses but a lion, a giraffe, and a deer. There are two chariots as well. Originally located at Coney Island, it was moved to Prospect Park in 1952, where it thrived for several decades. After a period of disrepair and closure in the 1980s, it was renovated, reopening in all its glory in 1990. Prospect Park is also the site of the Lefferts Homestead Historic House Children's Museum. The Lefferts House, a Dutch-American farmhouse, was built in the 1780s by Flatbush landowner Peter Lefferts. The City of New York acquired it in 1918 and moved it to the park from its original site several blocks away. It's open seasonally; call 718-965-6505 for information about events and activities.

Prospect Park is not hard to get to, whether by car or by public transportation. The 2 subway will take you to Grand Army Plaza, which is itself well worth seeing before you enter the park; or you can take the F train to the 15th Street Prospect Park station, or the Q train to the Prospect Park stop. It's also easy to travel within the park, thanks to the free "Heart of Brooklyn" trolley, which runs on weekends and holidays from noon to 6 PM. The Wollman Center and Rink is its first stop, and from there it makes stops throughout the park at attractions such as the Picnic House and the Bandshell. It also stops near the Brooklyn Museum of Art and the Brooklyn Botanic Garden.

The Lefferts House in Prospect Park is old, but there is an even older house in Brooklyn, this one in the Flatlands section of southeast Brooklyn. The **Peter Claesen Wyckoff House and Museum** (5902 Clarendon Road at Ralph Avenue, 718-629-5400; www.wyckoffassociation.org) was built in the early 1650s and is considered the oldest house in New York City. A National Historic Landmark, it is maintained and managed by the Wyckoff

Association, which operates it as a living-history museum of the early Dutch experience in America.

For all its charm, there's one thing Prospect Park does not have, and that's the Manhattan skyline (though if you take the subway there you get a wonderful view of Manhattan on the elevated portion of the F train). It is hard to match the movie-magic image of Central Park, with the view of the Fifth Avenue, Central Park West, and Central Park South skylines seen through leaves and branches. When two unique destinations near Prospect Park are added into the equation, though, Prospect Park becomes an ideal component of a major Brooklyn day trip. The Brooklyn Botanic Garden and the Brooklyn Museum are both special enough to justify a trip from almost anywhere within day-trip range.

Publicity about the **Brooklyn Museum of Art** (200 Eastern Parkway, 718-638-5000; www.brooklynart.org) veers between the minimal and the sensational. In 1999, one of the works on display at the traveling the "Sensations" exhibit incorporated elephant dung, generating controversy and publicity. A few years before that, another special exhibit, "The Impressionists in Winter," brought in crowds, almost universally appreciative, to wander the galleries and gaze at dozens of idyllic landscapes. But even when there is no timely or well-reviewed special exhibit at the museum, it's a treasure house of art history—the second-largest art museum in New York, outranked in size only by the Metropolitan Museum of Art—and it even looks important. The present building, dating to the 1890s, was designed by McKim, Mead & White, and it has the monumental dignity you'd expect. Inside, apart from the heavily populated special exhibits, the exhibit galleries are often quiet, occasionally deserted.

The period rooms are among the museum's star attractions. There are more than two dozen of these rooms, and unless your visit coincides with a school trip or group tour, it's possible that you will have this richly detailed and highly evocative series of spaces to yourself. Here you can see the interior of a seventeenth-century Brooklyn-Dutch house, a room from a Rockefeller mansion that once stood in Manhattan, and many other vivid reminders of how people used to live. The museum is also known for its Egyptian art, African art, pre-Columbian art, and an extensive collection of American painting and sculpture.

The museum is easy to get to by subway, since the 2 train stops at the

Eastern Parkway/Brooklyn Museum stop. You can also drive to the museum and pay for parking, space permitting, in the museum's own lot.

The museum has a café; not far from the museum, **Tom's Restaurant** (782 Washington Street, at the corner of Sterling Place, 718-636-9738) is a popular and friendly luncheonette that serves breakfast and lunch.

The **Brooklyn Children's Museum** (145 Brooklyn Avenue at St. Mark's Avenue, 718-735-4400; www.brooklynkids.org) is a great place to bring children on a weekend or a day off from school. Founded in 1899, it bills itself as the world's oldest museum for children, and its collection now encompasses 20,000 cultural artifacts and natural-history specimens, including live plants and animals. In addition to being an interactive museum, designed to keep children entertained while teaching them about technology, nature, and the world around them, it offers a rich variety of school programs and family workshops. Getting there is also fun: there is free weekend trolley service to the museum from Grand Army Plaza, with a stop at the Brooklyn Museum of Art. Driving is an option, of course, though you can't necessarily count on the availability of on-street parking.

If you aren't in the mood for a museum, consider a prolonged stroll through the Brooklyn Museum of Art's dazzling outdoor neighbor, the **Brooklyn Botanic Garden** (Eastern Parkway, west of the Brooklyn Museum, 718-623-7200; www.bbg.org). Unlike parks, which can seem less impressive to people who live outside cities than they do to city dwellers, botanical gardens go far beyond the natural beauty to be found in most suburban yards. They are outdoor natural-history museums of a sort and worth visiting no matter how many trees you have in your yard. The Brooklyn Botanic Garden, with more than 50 acres, is impressive, albeit only about one-fifth the size of the New York Botanical Garden in the Bronx. Among the highlights are its Japanese Garden, with a cherry arbor that makes springtime visits especially appealing; the Cranford Rose Garden, with thousands of bushes and more than one thousand varieties of roses; and, unique to Brooklyn, a Celebrity Path, with stepping-stones inscribed with the names of famous Brooklynites, such as Mary Tyler Moore and Woody Allen.

The Garden was founded in 1910, and the Native Flora Garden dates to 1911. Features have been added at frequent intervals over the decades. For example, in 1925, thirty-two dwarf potted trees were donated, forming the nucleus of what is now a famous bonsai collection; the Folger Shakespeare Garden opened in that year as well. The present Shakespeare Garden, in the form of an English cottage garden, is the second one at the Botanic Garden and displays dozens of plants mentioned in Shakespeare's works. In 1979, it replaced the original one, which was heavily shaded by Austrian pine trees at the southern edge of the Children's Garden, founded in 1914 and the oldest continuously operated garden of its type in the world. The Steinhardt Conservatory greenhouse complex houses not only the C. V. Starr Bonsai Museum but also the usual enjoyable multiple-climate displays of plants that thrive in desert, tropical, and temperate zones.

The Brooklyn Botanic Garden is open year-round and is closed Mondays (except for holiday Mondays other than Labor Day); it is also closed Thanksgiving, Christmas, and New Year's Day. Adult admission is $3, and children under sixteen are admitted free. Refreshments and lunches are available at the Terrace Café. Like the Brooklyn Museum of Art, the garden is easily reached by subway (2 train to Eastern Parkway or Q train to Prospect Park). There is also a fairly reasonably priced parking lot ($12 maximum fee at this writing).

The **Brooklyn Academy of Music,** popularly known as BAM (ticket information, 718-636-4100; wwwbam.org), is a major cultural center, attracting audiences from throughout the metropolitan area. The wide scope of its arts programs makes it an inviting day or evening destination. Its main building at 30 Lafayette Street was built in 1908 and now houses the BAM Opera House, a café, and a multiscreen cinema; BAM's Harvey Theater is located nearby, at 651 Fulton Street, in another impressively restored building. **Junior's** (386 Flatbush Avenue Extension, 718-852-5257), a legendary deli/restaurant, is also in the neighborhood, making it convenient to enjoy great cheesecake and other traditional New York favorites before or after you attend a concert or other event at BAM.

There are people who feel the **Aquarium for Wildlife Conservation** (8th Street and Surf Avenue, 718-265-3474;

www.wcs.org/zoos) should also be on the must-visit list of Brooklyn places. Maybe. The aquarium, formerly known as the New York Aquarium, moved to Coney Island from Battery Park in Manhattan in 1957. And although it does not compare to the aquariums in Boston or Baltimore, it is the only one New York has. It boasts more than 10,000 specimens from about 300 species. Among its attractions are a replica of Pacific coast cliffs that provide a habitat for Pacific walruses, California sea otters, black-footed penguins, harbor seals, and other marine creatures; and Discovery, an indoor education and exhibit center where you can handle live specimens and generally enjoy hands-on exhibits as well as a variety of sea dwellers in tanks of various sizes.

Having seen the aquarium, you could stroll over to **Nathan's Famous** (1310 Surf Avenue at 15th Street, 718-946-2202; open year-round) and have a hot dog (or several). Yes, you can find Nathan's Famous at your local mall, but Nathan's was established at Coney Island in 1916, and you are visiting history when you eat here. Coney Island has a great past as a beach resort and amusement park; some people still love it, but it isn't for everyone. It looks somewhat scruffy and you need to be careful when you visit. It is easy to get to, though: the F, Q, and W trains go to Stillwell Avenue, and from there it's a short walk along or across Surf Avenue to what's left of Coney Island's festive soul. The F and Q trains also stop at the West 8th Street/NY Aquarium station.

East of Coney Island, you might want to explore Brighton Beach Avenue, with its bustling Russian community and vibrant commercial district in the shadow of the elevated tracks. It doesn't take more than a glance at the shop windows on Brighton Beach Avenue to realize that you have entered a very different world. Many of the signs are in the Cyrillic alphabet, and even the hand-lettered English prices at the produce stands are European in style, with crossed "7"s and spiky letters. There are bakeries selling Russian breads and pastries, as well as cafés, some with bilingual menus and some with menus only in Russian. The movie theater on Brighton Beach Avenue, just beyond the corner of Coney Island Avenue where the tracks turn inland to go toward Midwood and leave the avenue in almost disconcerting sunlight, has been there for decades. As a teenager, my husband used to walk there from his home in nearby Sheepshead Bay. Now the theater is called the Atlantic Oceana, and it shows Russian movies; the front of the theater is decorated with Russian movie posters and there's a Russian café on the premises as well. On several street corners, Russian paperbacks can be found for sale at outdoor bookstalls, completing the sense of having traveled to someplace far away and rather glamorous.

For as long as anyone can remember, the glory of Brighton Beach has been its proximity to the ocean. A luxury residential complex called Oceana, complete with penthouses, roof gardens, terraces, and a clubhouse, has gone up on the site of the Brighton Beach Baths—the swim club that thrived through much of the twentieth century. The surviving blocks of apartment buildings still get ocean breezes and, in some cases, ocean views; they add to the slightly frayed but generally comfortable atmosphere. As my husband and I recently walked along Coney Island Avenue toward the ocean and crossed a small side street a short block from the ocean, he remembered that Brightwater Court had always been considered a desirable place to live. We also noticed that the building at the corner of Coney Island Avenue and Brightwater Court has colorful, elaborate art-deco trim in addition to its standard respectable brick facade.

Of course, you can't have an urban oceanfront without a boardwalk, and the Brighton Beach boardwalk is part of a long and popular one that goes to Coney Island and beyond. The Brighton Beach section is a place where people sit, gaze and talk, while others stroll, bike, or run. Years ago, when my husband was spending more summer days than he wanted to at Brighton Beach, the talk was a largely a blend of English and Yiddish, divided to some extent along generational lines. In the late spring of 2002, almost everyone, old, middle-aged, and young, was speaking Russian. There were still many elderly people taking the sun and the sea air, the men in caps and the women in head scarves; there were lots of small children romping and bouncing balls, and a few noticeable outsiders like us, just walking or biking, playing tourist. The buildings that once housed arcades and establishments dispensing hot-dogs and soft ice cream are now outdoor cafés—with indoor sections for inclement weather and evocative names such as the **Winter Garden Restaurant, Café Moscow,** and **Tatiana**. Especially concentrated along the boardwalk between Brighton 6th Street and Brighton 4th Street, some are better known as late-night supper clubs. The outdoor tables, just beginning to be occupied when we walked along the boardwalk around noon on a sunny Sunday, all featured intricately folded napkins tucked into wine glasses. One restaurant had a purple and lavender color scheme, another an equally spring-like blue and yellow. The menus, in Russian and English, were similar to each other, listing borscht, shish-kebab, and a variety of other Russian dishes. There were still windows at which hungry passersby could purchase soft ice cream—brightened by posters advertising colorful ice cream confections with Russian names.

Leaving the boardwalk we headed for a familiar landmark that hasn't changed and still evokes the other Brighton Beach of an earlier wave of Eastern European immigrants—**Mrs. Stahl's Knishes** (1001 Brighton Beach Avenue, 718-648-0210), at the corner of Brighton Beach and Coney Island Avenues. It opened in 1935, and my husband assured me that the boxes and string that were used to package our purchases hadn't changed since his 1950s memories of the place. The knishes we brought home were still good when we microwaved them for a late lunch.

Getting to Brighton Beach is easy by car or by public transportation. The D and Q subways stop at Brighton Beach, and Coney Island Avenue is a clearly marked exit off the Belt Parkway. We drove in on a Sunday morning and found a parking space right on Coney Island Avenue across from the vacant hardware store that once belonged to my husband's uncle. If you don't find a parking space on the street, there's a parking lot just off the boardwalk on Brighton 4th Street; it may get very crowded late at night or on beach days, but it was almost entirely empty on a spring Sunday.

18

Queens:
Stadium Culture

■   ■   ■   ■   ■   ■   ■   ■   ■   ■

Queens doesn't have skyscrapers, but it has great skyline views. It doesn't have an aura of international glamour, but it's renowned for its everyday ethnic diversity. In many ways, it is everything Manhattan is not: sprawling instead of compact, low-rise rather than high-rise. It has numbered streets, avenues, roads, and places, in a grid that is logical but more complicated than the straightforward rectangles of most of Manhattan. Parts of Queens—Astoria, Long Island City—are a few minutes from Manhattan by subway; others—Kew Gardens, Forest Hills, Bayside—are not much farther away but are deliberately suburban in style, marked by exits on Robert Moses–era parkways or Tudor-style stations on the Long Island Railroad.

Some things about Queens are perennial: the blocks of homes of all sizes and styles, the abundance of cars, the fabled cemeteries with even more fabled views of Manhattan. In addition to the compelling fabric of everyday life, there are also some special places and events that lend themselves to day-tripping.

The most stellar Queens event is the U.S. Open. Played until the late 1970s at the West Side Tennis Club in Forest Hills and now played at the **USTA National Tennis Center** (Flushing Meadows–Corona Park, 718-760-6200) in Flushing, this legendary tennis tournament spans the weeks immediately before and after Labor Day weekend. It is a wonderfully satisfying day

out, whether or not you play tennis. The ball goes back and forth rhythmi-
cally, the players swoop, the crowd applauds. It's both restful and exciting.
The first week of the Open, which is also the last week of school vacation for
most metropolitan-area schools, makes a particularly appealing day trip for
school-age children who like to play tennis and have the patience to spend
hours watching others play tennis. Tickets go on sale in June of each year,
and sometimes grounds passes sell out well before the event; night tickets for
the opening week usually stay available until closer to the event. The first
time I went, though, I bought my grounds pass for the first Friday that very
day at the U. S. Tennis Center box office. My children had been given tickets to the Open, complete with decent seats at Arthur Ashe Stadium and a
pass for good, free parking. So I drove them in, waited on line for a long but
bearable amount of time, got a ticket for myself, and had a wonderful time.
There is an added glamour the second week, with the excitement of the later
rounds and the concentration of famous players, famous spectators, and
surprise late-round survivors.

A grounds pass lets you spend the entire day, from 11 AM until the last
match ends, watching tennis and people everywhere except for Arthur Ashe
Stadium. A day ticket for Arthur Ashe admits you to all matches, not just those
that are played at the big stadium (and it is very big—from seats in the Upper
Promenade, the players look, if not like ants, like very small toy figures). Not
having a seat at Ashe means you will miss a few top-seeds, but during the first
week you can see many well-known players and lots of interesting less-known
ones on the outer courts. My daughter especially likes watching doubles
matches on the small courts with just a few bleacher seats, where you are about
as close to the players as you would be at a high-school match—but the unher-
alded players you are watching are world-class nonetheless.

The food is incredibly expensive, but it tastes good. I had a delicious
"small" glass of fresh lemonade on a searingly hot August day at the 2001
Open for $4.50. My $7 spinach-and-mushroom crepe was excellent too. My
daughter really enjoyed her individual barbecued-chicken pizza for a little
over $8. Her friend Katie, who had recently had her wisdom teeth removed,
settled for easy-to-eat luxury-priced soup. We did eventually decide to refill
the $4.50 Evian bottles at water fountains though. One year we developed a
great enthusiasm for the waffle fries sold both at the Arthur Ashe concession
booth and in the open food court; though not the basis for a well-balanced
meal, they are very good, relatively economical, and filling.

To get to Flushing Meadows, you can drive or take public transportation. Traffic can be very heavy, but parking is not a major problem. If the Mets are not playing at home, the Shea Stadium parking lots are available, and the walk from there to the Open is easy and lined by reassuring numbers of police officers. It is also a simple matter to take the subway from Grand Central Station to the Willets Point–Shea Stadium station on the 7 line. If you are commuting via Penn Station, the easiest route is the Long Island Railroad; take the Port Washington line from Penn Station to Shea Stadium. You can also take the E, F, N, or R and change to the 7 in Queens.

To get tickets to the Open, be alert for notices advising the public that tickets will be going on sale on a given date (usually early June). They're available by phone and on-line through TicketMaster, or you can make the trip to the box office at the Tennis Center, and get them in person. (Incidentally, the National Tennis Center is the largest public tennis facility in the world, with 33 courts available for the public to play on during much of the year. For a different kind of tennis day trip in Queens, call the National Tennis Center for fee and court-reservation information.)

Flushing Meadows offers more than tennis. From the top row of Arthur Ashe Stadium, you get a great view of Shea Stadium, home of the Mets. Leaving the Tennis Center Gate opposite the main entrance to Arthur Ashe Stadium, you also get a fine vista of the Unisphere, a relic of the 1964–65 World's Fair. To people who are old enough to remember having visited the 1964–65 World's Fair, this 140-foot-tall stainless-steel sculpture is likely to evoke instant memories of Belgian waffles, which were the culinary high point of the World's Fair for many teenage visitors. Flushing Meadows also hosted the 1939–40 World's Fair.

What's left to see in Flushing Meadows other than a few relics of the fairs? The **New York Hall of Science** (111th Street at 46th Avenue, 718-699-0005; www.nyhallsci.org), for one. This is a real science museum, with 225 exhibits, many of them interactive and designed to delight young visitors who like museums that let them handle things. As my daughter used to ask, "Are there buttons?" At the Hall of Science, the answer is yes; if not buttons, handles, knobs, computers, even bells and whistles (or at least an interactive exhibit called Sound Sensations—the Inside Story of Audio).

The building that houses the Hall of Science was originally a pavilion at the 1964–65 World's Fair and became a museum in 1966. It has undergone several renovations and expansions since then, culminating in 1997 with the

30,000-square-foot outdoor Science Playground, which is intended to bring physics to life for children ages six and older. Among the playground's attractions are a 3-D spider web, giant slides, windmills, an Archimedes screw on which to make water flow upward, light-activated kinetic sculpture, and a giant teeter-totter. The playground is open from April 1 to November 31, weather permitting, and there is an additional $2 admission fee per person.

There is also plenty to entertain and enlighten a family inside the museum. Exhibits include Marvelous Molecules, featuring a thirty-five-foot-long glucose molecule and an infrared camera to map out hot spots in your body. The Pfizer Foundation Biochemistry Discovery Lab provides an opportunity to find out what makes the ocean foam and roses red, as well as much more about the chemistry of living things. In Hidden Kingdoms—the World of Microbes, visitors step through the twelve-foot-tall eye of a sewing needle to view a collection of microbes, the world's smallest living creatures. At Seeing the Light, 91 exhibits allow visitors to experiment with light, color, and perception, via such classic kid-pleasing activities as blowing giant soap bubbles and casting a colorful shadow.

The New York Hall of Science is open daily and there is an admission fee for nonmembers. If you are traveling by subway, take the 7 train to the 111th Street station. The Hall is accessible by car from the Long Island Expressway 108th Street exit, or the eastbound Grand Central Parkway Midtown Tunnel exit. Parking is available.

A few blocks away is another child-friendly attraction—the **Queens Wildlife Center** (53-51 111th Street at 53rd Avenue, 718-271-7761; www.wcs.org). This zoo, established in 1968, reopened in 1992 after renovation by the Wildlife Conservation Society in partnership with the New York City Department of Parks and Recreation. Habitats include the Great Plains, the rocky California coast, and a Northeast forest; they are home to a number of American species, such as American bison, mountain lions, California sea lions, American bald eagles, and Roosevelt elk. The Wildlife Center is also home to South American species, including spectacled bears. There is also an aviary in the form of a geodesic dome designed by Buckminster Fuller and originally used in the 1964–65 World's Fair. The zoo is accessible via the 7 subway train to 111th Street and by car from the Long Island Expressway 108th Street exit and the eastbound Grand Central Parkway Midtown Tunnel exit. It is open every day of the year, and admission in late 2001 was $2.50 for adults, 50 cents for children aged three to twelve.

There is yet another attraction at Flushing Meadows, this one artistic rather than scientific. The **Queens Museum of Art** (718-592-9700) features a 9,000-square-foot-plus model of all five boroughs of New York City, made for the 1964–65 World's Fair and still dazzling after all these years. It was created on a scale of one inch per hundred feet and includes all sorts of buildings from skyscrapers to tenements. The museum is open Wednesday through Sunday, and there is a $4 suggested donation.

Everyone knows about the **New York Mets,** and most people love them—especially during good times like the successful 2000 season. Still, the Mets don't have to be in the postseason whirl to be fun to watch. An afternoon or evening at **Shea Stadium** (123-01 Roosevelt Avenue, Flushing, 718-507-METS/6387; for tickets, call 718-507-TIXX/8499) is a part of the New York experience.

Getting to Shea Stadium is surprisingly easy by subway or car. I remember my pleasant surprise the first time we drove a group of fourth-grade boys there from northern New Jersey, via the George Washington Bridge and the Triborough Bridge. The parking lot is vast, and although getting in and out involves dealing with traffic, once you are out of the initial crunch the congestion isn't usually too painful. Shea Stadium opened in 1964, the year after the Mets joined the National League, and my husband and I both remember doing homework as we listened (separately, in different parts of the metropolitan area) to Mets games during their first few error-laden years, so their occasional dramatic postseason successes have a particular resonance in our family.

Queens is also a vast collection of diverse neighborhoods populated by virtually every ethnic group imaginable. It's also a part of the city with a very long history. American Indians lived there before European settlers came; in the 1630s, Dutch farmers were tending cattle and raising crops, to be followed within a decade or so by English settlers. The agricultural tradition didn't end until well into the twentieth century. Queens was a place of farms, villages, and small towns until the subways were built to connect it to the rest of the city in the early decades of the twentieth century. It is still full of neighborhoods worth exploring. Astoria, for example, is a vibrant community with a large Greek population and a generous share of tempting restaurants and bakeries, especially along Broadway, just a short walk from the Broadway station of the N train. For a person with self-control or no sweet tooth, it may be enough just to gaze through the window of the **Omonia Cafe** (32-20 Broadway, 718-274-6650). For most others, a stop will be necessary, either to indulge on the spot or to buy a box of goodies to take home. You could be relatively restrained and buy some kourambiedes (almond crescents) coated with powdered sugar, or you could be truly shameless and get a selection of richly filled and decorated pastries. Or you could compromise and get some of almost everything. You can eat a full meal nearby, too; **Uncle George's** (33-19 Broadway, 718-626-0593) and **Syros Seafood** (32-11 Broadway, 718-278-1877) are reasonably priced Greek favorites; a couple of blocks away is **Karyatis** (35-03 Broadway, 718-204-0666).

Enjoying Greek food and pastries may be only a secondary part of a trip to Astoria for some people. The neighborhood is, after all, home to the **American Museum of the Moving Image** (35th Avenue at 36th Street, 718-784-0077; www.ammi.org). If you love movies you will enjoy this museum. If you love movies in a serious way—can name more than one famous cinematographer, have ever taken a film course that lasted at least a full semester, or have personal experience with video cameras—you will love the place. In fact, you will love not just the museum itself, but its location on the edge of a vibrant ethnic neighborhood and in the heart of seemingly endless blocks of warehouse-style structures that house the Kaufman Astoria Studios.

There was a time, shortly after World War I, when Queens was the center of the film industry, with more than twenty studios. Kaufman Astoria Studios are a living, fully functioning reminder of that era. The studios, originally known as the Astoria Studio, have been part of the entertainment industry since 1920. More than 100 silent films were shot there, the Marx Brothers made their first film there, Claudette Colbert and Edward G. Robinson, among others, made their first talkies there, and the studio was also home to Paramount Newsreels. The Army Signal Corps used the studios during World War II—and for decades after—to make training films and features.

Civilian production returned in 1975; the studio was named a National Historic Landmark in 1976, and reopened in 1977. During the 1980s it underwent a major expansion and became known as the Kaufman Astoria Studios. It is now a state-of-the-art production center, with six stages, including the largest one east of Los Angeles; a lighting and grip company; an audio recording and post production studio; and more. Movies and television shows continue to be shot here, and it is home to Lifetime Television and WFAN.

The American Museum of the Moving Image can be a challenging destination, exciting or daunting depending on your mindset and your companions. Its mission is to educate the public "about the art, history, technique, and technology of film, television, and digital media, and to [examine] their impact on culture and society." It has the nation's largest permanent collection of moving-image artifacts, and it offers a variety of screenings, demonstrations, and other programs.

I visited it early one Wednesday afternoon by myself—and I don't just mean without a companion. I had the entire place to myself, except for security guards. That made me feel less self-conscious about enjoying some of the interactive exhibits, but it also made the whole place seem a bit overwhelming and forlorn. I did appreciate the opportunity to be the voice of the sweet young pig in a scene from *Babe* in total privacy; on weekends there must be lines for this kind of treat.

That interactive exhibit was part of the museum's core exhibit, "Behind the Screen," a large and varied compilation of interactive computer-assisted activities, artifacts, installations, and other materials. There are also regular demonstrations of animation and film editing for visitors who wish to delve more deeply into the various processes involved in production, marketing, and exhibition of moving images. However, fully appreciating and understanding the finer points of the many cameras and other pieces of equipment required somewhat more focus and effort than I was prepared for. I did especially enjoy the nineteenth-century galloping-horse motion studies by Edweard Muybridge, which I remember learning about in a long-ago art-history class.

"King Tut's Movie Palace" is a colorful work of art by Red Grooms and Lysiane Luong in the form of a stylized movie palace. Even when historic films are not being shown on its screen, it is a treat well worth admiring. The display of toys and games related to movies and television shows is probably a crowd-pleaser, too, though since there were no other visitors when I was there, I can't judge the general reaction. I enjoyed having room and leisure to admire the collection of colorful, highly stylized fan-magazine covers, tucked away in back of one of the galleries.

The museum is open Tuesday through Friday from noon to 5 PM, Saturday and Sunday from 11 AM to 6 PM. Admission is $8.50 for adults, $4.50 for children, and $5.50 for senior citizens and college students with student identification. "Behind the Screen" exhibit tours are offered at 2 PM for no additional charge. The museum has both a shop and a café and is a pleasant walk from either the Broadway stop of the N train or the Steinway Street stop of the R train.

The American Museum of the Moving Image is just one of several institutions that are increasingly making Queens a place for serious museum going, especially for people who really know and care about modern art. While the Museum of Modern Art's Manhattan building undergoes major renovation (see chapter 10, "Great Manhattan Museums"), parts of its collection are temporarily housed in the borough, near P.S. 1 Contemporary Art Center. The rebuilding is expected to be completed in 2005; in the meantime, **MoMA QNS** (33rd Street at Queens Boulevard, 212-708-9400) will be the place to see some of what you would ordinarily visit on West 53rd Street. The Queens Artlink, established in 2001, is a courtesy weekend shuttle service that makes it even easier to take advantage of these impressive destinations. One route runs from the Museum of Modern Art on West 53rd Street between Fifth and Sixth Avenues to MoMA QNS. Another route connects MoMA QNS, P.S. 1 Contemporary Art Center, the Isamu Noguchi Garden Museum, the Socrates Sculpture Park, and the American Museum of the Moving Image. Call 212-708-9750 for information.

P.S. 1 Contemporary Art Center (22-25 Jackson Avenue at 46th Avenue, Long Island City, 718-784-2084; www.ps1.org) is affiliated with MoMA. As you might expect, it is indeed an old school building. Construction of the red-brick structure was completed in the early 1890s, and a wing was added in 1906. The school was distinguished by its large stone clock tower and brass bell. By the 1950s, the school was considered troubled. In 1963 students and teachers were transferred to other schools throughout the area, and in 1964 the clock tower was demolished. After serving for years as a warehouse, the building was closed in 1974 but preserved through the efforts of a community coalition that proposed its reuse as a community resource. The city gave the building to the newly formed Institute for Art and Resources, which reopened the structure in 1976. There are galleries and display spaces throughout the building as well as outside it; the changing program of exhibits focuses on the innovative and unexpected.

At the **Isamu Noguchi Garden Museum** (32-37 Vernon Boulevard at 33rd Road, Long Island City, 718-721-1932; www.noguchi.org), the striking setting was created by the artist himself. Thirteen galleries are housed in a converted factory; the garden in the middle contains granite and basalt sculptures. The exhibit includes more than 250 works by Noguchi (1904–1988) and is operated by the Isamu Noguchi Foundation, Inc.

The nearby **Socrates Sculpture Park** (Vernon Boulevard at Broadway, Long Island City, 718-956-1819) was once an illegal dump. In 1985 it was turned into a public art park displaying large-scale outdoor sculpture. Admission is free, and the park is open daily.

Cutting-edge as the Queens art world may be, there are still visible traces of an older, more traditional Queens. First, there are the distinctive residential areas. **Sunnyside Gardens,** for example, was an early planned community and is now on the National Register of Historic Places. **Forest Hills Gardens,** farther east, was built in a deliberately picturesque style to appeal to affluent home buyers and apartment renters. At about the same time and not far away, developers were building **Kew Gardens** with Tudor-style houses and luxurious apartments. The model workers' housing and more ambitious homes of **Steinway** reflect another aspect of residential development; it was built in the 1870s as a company town for the Steinway piano factory; the workers' row houses as well as the Steinway mansion and factory are still there.

There are also very old houses in Queens, surviving reminders of much earlier days. In addition to their architectural appeal, some have specific historical significance. The **John Bowne House** (37-01 Bowne Street, Flushing, 718-359-0528), for example, built in 1661, isn't just one of the oldest buildings in the United States and an interesting example of Dutch-English vernacular architecture. Although much of the structure has remained unchanged since 1830, it is especially important as a symbol of religious freedom. When a group of English Quakers came to Flushing (then known as Vlissengen) in 1657, Governor Peter Stuyvesant banned all but Dutch Reformed religious observances. Despite this, John Bowne allowed his home to be used as a place for Quaker meetings. Bowne was imprisoned, banished, and made his way to Amsterdam, where he apparently persuaded the Council of the Dutch West India Company to order Stuyvesant to permit all religions to be practiced freely in New Amsterdam. The Bowne House continued to serve as a Quaker meeting house until late in the seventeenth century. The house is open Tuesday, Saturday, and Sunday from 2:30 PM to 4:30 PM.

The **Kingsland Homestead** (143-35 37th Avenue, Flushing, 718-939-0647), built about 1785 by Charles Doughty, the son of a wealthy Quaker, is now the home of the Queens Historical Society. There are exhibits about Queens history on the first floor; a parlor on the second floor reflects the lifestyle of a middle-class Victorian family. The Kingsland Homestead is very close to the Bowne House and its hours are the same. This is not quite the homestead's original location: in 1923, when a subway extension threatened to destroy the house, it was moved, and in 1968, when construction threatened it again, it was moved again.

The **Queens County Farm Museum** (73-50 Little Neck Parkway, Floral Park, Queens, 718-347-3276) is a pleasant destination for families who live in Nassau County. The farmhouse is open only on weekends, although the grounds, which include orchards and fields, are open daily.

The city has beaches as well as art and history. In fact, the **Gateway National Recreation Area** (718-318-4340), which spans parts of New York and New Jersey, includes three areas in Queens—one classic recreational beach and two natural areas. **Breezy Point,** at the western end of the Rockaway Peninsula, is a place for fishing and bird-watching. The 9,000-acre **Jamaica Bay Wildlife Refuge,** another great place for bird-watching, also offers more than five miles of trails. **Jacob Riis Park,** on the Rockaway peninsula, has a mile of beach and boardwalk, as well as a variety of other facilities such as ball fields and a pool. The park also offers facilities for softball, baseball, football, rugby, paddleball and handball. Riis Park, with its distinctive outdoor clock and handsome 1930s bathhouse, is listed on the National Register of Historic Places. Both Breezy Point and

Riis Park are well west of the last stop of the A or S train and are best reached by car. The Jamaica Bay Wildlife Refuge is near the Broad Channel station on the A or S train.

19

Staten Island:
Yes, It Is Part of New York

Once, the mystique of not having a bridge connecting it to the rest of New York City made Staten Island seem like a faraway place—and that's still the case if you're trying to get there from Manhattan; from there Staten Island can be reached by the traditional, romanticized, and very practical Staten Island Ferry. Several bridges connect Staten Island to places other than Manhattan, though. Starting with the Bayonne Bridge in the north, with the Goethals Bridge in the middle and Outerbridge Crossing providing a connection surprisingly far south, you can make the trip from Hudson, Union, and Middlesex counties in New Jersey so easily that it may make you wonder why Staten Island is part of New York. Perhaps the most significant bridge, though, is the Verrazano Narrows Bridge, which links Staten Island to Brooklyn and thus to the rest of the city and to the road network of all of Long Island. It's been decades since the bridge was built—it opened in late 1964—and the density of development since then is evidence of the impact road connections had on the borough's economy and way of life. Once you reach the island, if you are driving, you can wander surface streets or take Route 278 (the Staten Island Expressway) to the various exits leading to your chosen attractions. If you've arrived by ferry, city buses take you where you need to go, but you can also ride the trains of Staten Island Rapid Transit (SIRT), an elevated rail line.

There are a number of intriguing, even unique, spots to explore; they may not be at the top of the New York City tour list, but they're worth an excursion or two. My husband focuses on the Staten Island Zoo, especially its large collection of snakes. The zoo is relatively small, but the snake collection and some of the snakes themselves are relatively large. I prefer the historical sites, Historic Richmond Town and the Alice Austen House. The Snug Harbor Cultural Center is a dazzling array of nineteenth-century buildings, now highlighted by such attractions as the Noble Maritime Collection and the Staten Island Children's Museum.

Only decades ago, Staten Island looked almost like country. There were lots of old houses, village-like commercial districts, and greenery. Interestingly, though, some of Staten Island's current main attractions weren't yet developed. Snug Harbor was there of course, as it has been since the nineteenth century, but it was in a state of relative neglect, caught between its original role as a home for retired sailors and its contemporary role as a center for the arts. The historic buildings of Richmond Town hadn't yet been brought to a central location and refurbished to become a living reflection of the borough's past. And the Alice Austen House, overlooking Upper New York Bay, was largely forgotten, as Alice Austen was for much of the twentieth century.

A visit to **Historic Richmond Town** (441 Clarke Avenue, 718-351-1611; www.historicrichmondtown.org) provides an effective introduction to the increasingly distant past of both Staten Island and New York City. It's easy to forget how pretty Staten Island used to be, with rolling hills, water views, and small towns that perfectly fit the ideal of small-town America in, say, 1888. Richmond Town is a village/museum complex centered around the old County Courthouse, a massive Greek Revival–style building. The complex is a joint project of the Staten Island Historical Society and the City of New York, which owns the land and buildings and partially funds the operations. Some of the homes and other structures in the complex are original to the site, part of the community that centered around the courthouse; others were moved from various parts of Staten Island. About half a dozen of the buildings are open to the public. The interiors of the others are closed, but their exteriors reflect a range of rural and small-town architecture. It's open year-round, but during July and August, numerous costumed "residents" provide not only information but also scheduled demonstrations of everything from cooking to dressing for a ball to celebrating Independence

Day. Special events at other times of year, some of which require advance reservations, include pumpkin picking at Decker Farm, a December candlelight tour, and a New Year's Ball. From September through June, Historic Richmond Town is open Wednesday through Sunday from 1 PM to 5 PM; in July and August, it opens at 10 AM Wednesday through Saturday, and at 1 PM on Sunday.

You can take the S74 bus from the St. George ferry slip to Richmond Town, or you can drive; there's ample parking. Whatever your mode of modern transportation, it will take you through a Staten Island streetscape of malls and (mostly) twentieth-century housing developments; occasionally blocks have a more 1940s or 1950s feeling with scattered older commercial buildings; it looks so much like a stereotypical suburb that the sight of MTA buses seems incongruous.

The streets immediately surrounding Richmond Town are tree-lined, with homes that suggest the early twentieth century. But as soon as you enter the visitor center, housed in the elegant and very nineteenth-century courthouse, the world is transformed. You walk in the door at what turns out to be the back of the courthouse, pay the very reasonable admission charge ($4 for adults; $2.50 for students, senior citizens, and children aged six to eighteen; admission is free for children under six and for Staten Island Historical Society members), and walk down the steps from the much more impressive front of the building. A small town, with a general store, neatly shuttered homes, and staff members in period costume, awaits you. Because not all of its structures are original to the site, Richmond Town blends reality and fantasy to some extent. The most interesting buildings are the ones that belonged there from the beginning, but the overall effect is a haunting reminder of a vanished place and time. The Stephens-Black House, built in 1837, is across the street from the courthouse, as it always has been. Its front parlor is especially gracious, with the mood set by a lovely marble-topped table. The rooms on the main floor are furnished in the style of the mid-nineteenth century; a sewing room, complete with an 1860s sewing machine and many fabric and needlework samples, provides insight into the way women of the era spent much of their time. The general store that occupies an ell behind the house, was, according to one of the very pleasant and seemingly well-informed docents, reconstructed based upon the recollections of Mr. Stephens's great-granddaughter. The wood counters and the assortment of goods on display look appropriately aged.

Down the hill, the Guyon-Lake-Tysen House is also open to the public. This Dutch farmhouse was moved from the community of New Dorp; on an exceptionally hot August morning, it was surprisingly comfortable inside, partly because the kitchen fireplace hadn't yet been lit and partly, according to one of the costumed docents, because the thick stone and plaster walls are good insulators. It was also designed to be well ventilated, with classic Dutch doors at the front and back of the center hallway half open to the breeze. The house was built in 1740 and much of its original woodwork survives.

Across Arthur Kill Road from the main village, the Voorlezer's House is said to be the oldest schoolhouse surviving in the United States. Built in 1695, it feels appreciably older than the pleasant homes across the road; the walls are less smooth, the windows smaller, the furnishings sparser and not as nice. The structure, built by the Dutch Reformed Church, served not only as a schoolhouse but also as a church and as the home of the minister/schoolmaster. This National Historic Landmark is the oldest of Richmond Town's original on-site buildings.

One of the most impressive buildings is a lovely brick edifice with a brownstone plaque above the front door; carving on the plaque identifies this as the County Clerk and Surrogates Office 1848. It was converted to a museum in 1934. Now it is the Historical Museum at Richmond Town, with well-displayed artifacts of Staten Island's past, from oystering and farming to beer brewing and brick making. It's a very pleasant as well as informative spot.

Richmond Town is a great place for a family or school trip. It gives a clear and accessible sense of the past, and if you time the visit right you can see demonstrations of open-hearth cooking and other chores and crafts. Richmond Town's setting and particular role—its brochure describes it as New York City's Historical Village—are unusual enough to be worth a trip for adults who enjoy a bit of time-traveling.

A nice footnote to the Richmond Town visit is an excursion to the **Alice Austen House Museum and Garden** (2 Hylan Boulevard, 718-816-4506). Alice Austen (1855–1952) was a photographer who recorded life around her everywhere, not just in New York but as far afield as Chicago's 1893 Columbian Exposition to even Bavaria. She grew up and lived in this cottage, which is literally on the shore of the Narrows, which connect Upper and Lower New York Bay. The home, called Clear Comfort by the Austen family, is an eighteenth-century farmhouse that was remodeled as a picturesque cottage by Alice Austen's grandparents. For much of her life, Alice Austen lived there in comfort, when she wasn't traveling. After losing her savings in the stock-market crash of 1929, she eventually had to sell the house and move to a city-run poorhouse.

With its gingerbread trim and diamond-paned windows, the house is a delightful surprise, even if you know about it ahead of time. It's on the water block of Hylan Boulevard off Bay Street, with a view of Manhattan, a closer view of Brooklyn, and a closer-still view of the Verrazano Narrows Bridge and whatever tankers and barges are in the Narrows and Bay at the time of your visit. Inside, you can see an exhibit of some of Austen's photographs, as well as the very cozy rooms themselves; the fully furnished parlor is especially delightful.

It's a particular treat to stand on the sloping lawn in front of Clear Comfort and watch the water of the Narrows slap against the shore a few yards away. The house is easily recognizable in pictures taken a century ago by Austen, although the water traffic is different and the surroundings were more rural then. Now, a relatively tall apartment building with lots of balconies dominates that block of Hylan Boulevard, although there are also about a dozen houses on the street.

After a period of neglect, Clear Comfort and the garden surrounding it were restored to their 1890s appearance. The house is designated as a Historic House of the New York City Department of Parks and Recreation and the site is operated by the Friends of Alice Austen House. The house is open Thursday through Sunday from noon to 5 PM, and the admission fee is $2. It doesn't take very long to see everything at the Alice Austen House and Garden, but a visit there is special nonetheless.

If you drive from Richmond Town to Snug Harbor, or for any other reason find yourself on the perimeter of the island along Kill Van Kull, you may at some point get an extraordinary view of the **Bayonne Bridge,** which is very slender and very tall, at least as seen from street level along Richmond Terrace. Its semicircular shape makes it look like a giant, free-standing protractor, and although it may be as prone to traffic tie-ups and annoyances as any other metropolitan-area bridge, it's a surprisingly elegant sight, worth appreciating as you head toward more traditional destinations.

Snug Harbor Cultural Center (1000 Richmond Terrace, 718-448-2500; www.snug-harbor.org), a National Historic Landmark, is a great cultural resource for Staten Islanders and visitors, but it's especially interesting because of what it was and what it still looks like. Unlike Richmond Town, it is an assemblage of buildings on their original sites; it's their function rather than their placement that has changed.

Originally called Sailor's Snug Harbor, it was built as a home for retired sailors, funded by an 1801 bequest from a businessman named Robert Richard Randall, whose father had been a privateer. Minard Lefever designed the first major buildings at Snug Harbor in Greek Revival style; eventually there were dozens of buildings in varying architectural styles on the grounds, including dormitories, barns, even a vaudeville house. Sailor's Snug Harbor opened in 1833, and by 1900 was home to about 1,000 elderly seamen. When the population declined to about 200 by the 1950s, the trustees of Sailor's Snug Harbor began to demolish some of the buildings. At its first meeting, the newly established New York City Landmarks Preservation Commission designated several of the twenty surviving buildings as city landmarks, and eventually the city purchased the entire site. In 1976 it became the Snug Harbor Cultural Center, which is now home to a variety of cultural institutions.

What you will see at first glance is a collection of great old buildings of various shapes and sizes, set on more than 80 acres of what is now parkland. Specific cultural attractions include the **Staten Island Children's Museum** (718-273-2060), with the hands-on exhibits children have come to expect and enjoy, and the **Newhouse Center for Contemporary Art**, which is housed in Main Hall, the oldest building on the site. The **Noble Maritime Collection** (718-447-6490; www.noblemaritime.org; admission $3 for adults and $2 for senior citizens and children) opened in late 2000 in the Lefever-designed Building D. In addition to the exhibits of paintings and maritime artwork (as well as a permanent exhibit about Sailor's Snug Harbor history), it's a treat to see the restored interior of this very impressive building. At this writing, Buildings A and B were undergoing major renovation so that the Staten Island Institute of Arts and Sciences could relocate to Snug Harbor from its present headquarters near the ferry terminal in St. George.

The **Staten Island Botanical Gardens** (718-273-8200), also on the grounds, include a greenhouse, a perennial garden, and the Pond Garden. One of the highlights is Connie Gretz's Secret Garden, a formal half-acre garden with a walled garden in the center modeled after the garden in *The Secret Garden*, Frances Hodgson Burnett children's classic. There is also a Chinese Scholar's Garden, modeled after a Ming Dynasty scholar's garden. Although you can explore most of the gardens freely, there are separate admission charges for the secret garden and the scholar's garden.

I first visited Snug Harbor in the mid-1980s when the adaptive reuse of the site hadn't progressed as far as it has now, and the buildings were clearly the stars. To me, they still are. The "Front Five," which include Building D and the Main Hall, are the Greek Revival centerpieces of the complex. Among my other favorites are the five mansard-roofed cottages on Cottage Road. On a smaller scale than some of the main buildings that run parallel to Richmond Terrace, the cottages are known as Cottage Row. They were built in the 1880s and have been gracefully renovated; now they are used for various administrative purposes; one serves as the Botanical Garden Visitor's Center.

Another special building is the **Music Hall**, built in 1893. It has a great porticoed front and a broad set of outside stairs in back where you can sit and look out at the Neptune Fountain. After decades of disuse, the hall was renovated in the 1990s and now hosts performances year-round. Across Chapel Road from the Music Hall, **Veterans Memorial Hall**, built as a chapel in 1856, now serves as a setting for concerts, recitals, and other events.

The cultural institutions and the year-round schedule of concerts and other special events are interesting, but it's the sum of the parts that really makes Snug Harbor worth the trip from outside Staten Island. Note, too, that the various museums do not have the same hours, and are not open daily, so you may find yourself wanting to visit the Noble Maritime Collection after enjoying the Botanical Gardens, but having to wait an hour or so until it opens—if it is open at all. Be sure to call and double-check opening times before you go if you are interested in visiting a particular building. And of course the same is true if you plan to attend a concert or other program; some are free and some require ticket purchases.

Snug Harbor's entrance isn't terribly well-marked; the signs are there but you won't see them from a distance. Once inside, there are small signs pointing to individual points of interest, but only after you find the Visitor's Center can you really orient yourself properly. At the Visitor's Center you can pick up a detailed sheet that will direct you on a self-guided walking tour, and that may be the best way to get an overview of Snug Harbor.

There are parking lots, but finding them is partly a matter of luck, since they are not prominently marked either. If you are not driving, you'll be glad to realize that the S40 bus runs right along Richmond Terrace, just outside the famous iron fence that separated Snug Harbor from the outside world. Snug Harbor is on the north shore of the island about two miles west of the ferry terminal.

Another reason to visit Staten Island is the **Staten Island Zoo** (614 Broadway, 718-442-3100; www.statenislandzoo.org). It is small enough to be manageable and not overwhelm small children or tired adults but varied enough to hold your interest. The reptile display in the Serpentarium boasts an especially extensive collection of North American rattlesnakes.

A state-of-the-art "African Savannah at Twilight" exhibit features animals native to the grasslands of central and southern Africa, including leopards, baboons, and lizards. The Ralph J. Lamberti Tropical Forest represents the flora and fauna of an endangered South American tropical forest. The N.Y. State Senator John J. Marchi Aquarium introduces visitors to a variety of marine creatures, from sharks to shrimp. The Children's Center, complete with a covered bridge and duck pond, may be less of a novelty to suburban visitors than to city visitors, but children will enjoy it all the same, and the center has the usual population of domestic farm animals. Throughout the zoo, a variety of outdoor exhibits such as a flamingo pool, freely roaming peacocks, and a pony track add to the pleasures of walking the zoo's grounds.

The Staten Island Zoo is easy to get to both from the Staten Island Expressway and by surface roads from Sailor's Snug Harbor. It is open daily except for Thanksgiving, Christmas Day, and New Year's Day; and admission is $3 for adults, $2 for children under twelve, and free for children under three and museum members.

Appendix A:
Getting There

A good map and a train or bus schedule will provide you with the basics of navigating the city. Depending upon which suburb you live in and where you are going, driving to the city makes sense, and a road map is the best guide. All you need after that is a convenient garage or good luck in your search for on-street parking. *(N.B.: Any time you park your car on the street in New York City or anywhere else you run some risk of a break-in or theft.)* The large garage on 42nd Street between Ninth and Tenth Avenues is ideally located for New Jersey visitors headed for Broadway theaters; the garage at the Metropolitan Museum of Art is enormous and well worth the money, whether you are going to the museum or elsewhere on the Upper East Side. Once you are parked and settled, you may want to turn to bus and subway travel within the city. Taxis are often the easiest way to travel and aren't necessarily less economical if you're in a group of three or four people and aren't going very far. For example, four people in a hurry to get to Penn Station from Fifth Avenue and 55th Street might very well do better to take a cab than to head for the nearest subway station; even with tip it probably won't cost much more, and unless traffic is heavy, it will be quick. In heavy traffic, though, cab rides become more expensive as the meter continues to run while the vehicle is at a standstill.

For Westchester, Connecticut, and Long Island commuters, the train has traditionally been a convenient choice for travel to

Manhattan, because so many towns have one-train service to Penn Station or Grand Central Terminal. For some New Jerseyans, that's also been the case, although for those of us who live in the Essex/Morris County corridor now served by NJ Transit's Midtown Direct, one-seat travel to New York's Penn Station is a relatively recent improvement. The old-fashioned version of the trip, taking the train to Hoboken and riding the ferry to Lower Manhattan, also has its benefits, even though economy of time isn't one of them. For schedules, routes, and rates, visit the respective agency Web sites: **www.mta.nyc.ny.us** or **www.njtransit.com.** Most subway stations also have free subway maps at the token booths.

Taking public transportation from your home to the city makes sense for a variety of reasons. Perhaps your destination is close to the train station, or you really dislike driving in the city; maybe you expect traffic to be heavy and parking at a premium. Public transportation removes worries about city parking, which may make up for the slightly cumbersome scheduling that train or bus travel involves. For example, taking the NY Waterway ferry to a Mets or Yankees game combines a touch of adventure with freedom from parking-lot panic, as long as you don't miss the boat. Taking the MTA's Metro-North and Long Island Railroad, or NJ Transit, then connecting with the city's own transportation system, is often surprisingly seamless; lots of subway lines connect with one train station or the other, adding to the feeling that in coming to New York you are sharing a traveling experience with people from all over the world. But you do have to keep your eye on the clock, or risk waiting an hour for your next train in or out of the city. And be sure the schedule you are using is up to date. As I write this, my son is sitting in Penn Station waiting for a 4:21 train when he thought he would be on a 3:42 train. The schedule, however, changed a week ago, and when he planned his visit home for a Memorial Day barbecue, neither of use realized there would be such a significant difference.

Once you reach the city, getting around is easy. First of all, it's a great place to walk. In Manhattan, north-south blocks are usually very short (twenty blocks to the mile), and east-west blocks are of variable length. Assuming reasonably acceptable weather, a walk of eight or ten north-south blocks can be very quick and pleasant, and if you enjoy walking, you can cover a lot more ground than that. For much of Manhattan, thanks to the logical numbered grid pattern of streets, you don't even need a map, just an address. Even so, there are exceptions to the easy-to-follow layout, notably in Lower Manhattan and Greenwich Village, where streets have interesting names and irregular angles. In the city's other four boroughs, a map or detailed directions to a specific destination are essential, because the streets generally have names rather than numbers. There is no substitute for simply knowing where a street is, and even where there are numbers, as in Queens, the numbering system isn't as easy to follow as it is in Manhattan. In some of the chapters, I've noted particularly convenient subway routes or places to park; in others, I've left transportation details to the reader, since there are so many variables, such as where you are coming from, how many people you are with, how mobile you are, and how familiar you are with a particular area. If you depend heavily on buses and subways, you probably already know about the wonders of the MetroCard. It is a great convenience that can save you a little money and offers a great deal of flexibility. Fare for either a bus or subway ride is $1.50, with free transfers within a two-hour period from bus to subway, subway to bus, and bus to bus. A Fun Pass gives you unlimited bus and subway rides for one day for $4. If you come to the city fairly often or have several people in your group, you might do better with a $15 MetroCard, which will give you eleven rides for the price of ten and will be good for about a year—and up to four people at a time are allowed to use it. You can get more information from the MTA Web site, or by calling 800-METROCARD/800-638-7622 from outside the city or 212-METRO-CARD/212-638-7622 from inside the city.

Bon voyage.

Appendix B:
Children in the City

You see children everywhere in the city; obviously, any place that's home to millions of people is also home to lots of children. But what about yours, the ones who don't live there? What's especially appealing for them—while appealing even more to you? Of course, much depends on the ages of your children, but your own interests play a large part in finding good activities and destinations for children. If you really like baseball, you might decide to introduce a preschooler to your sport at a Mets or Yankees game, but if not, you'll probably want to wait until the middle-elementary grades before embarking on this particular family outing. Similarly, if you love museums, you probably already know which museums allow strollers on weekends and which ones don't, which ones don't seem to mind babies in backpacks and which ones project a subtle sense of disapproval for the potential disturbance of their peace. New York is full of playgrounds in surroundings like Central Park or Prospect Park that impart a little glamour to the basic slide/swing/run routine.

Rather than put together a single citywide chapter of good places to go with children, many chapters mention destinations that work as well for children as for adults, or are specifically designed for children of particular ages. Among the prime destinations are the *Intrepid* and any boat ride; numerous museums, especially the American Museum of Natural History, the Metropolitan Museum of Art (Arms and Armor and Musical

Instruments in particular), and the Brooklyn Children's Museum; and the Bronx Zoo and the Central Park Zoo. There are more season-specific attractions as well; for example, children who like to ice skate will love a trip to the rink at Rockefeller Center. A trip to the theater, while at first thought an adult activity, in part because of the expense involved, can also be a wonderful family excursion if you choose your show carefully. Babies and toddlers can go pretty much anywhere if you're prepared to push their strollers or carry them. Children of middle-school age and older can go pretty much anywhere, too, depending on their interests. Shopping in SoHo, exploring South Street Seaport, going to the U.S. Open in Queens, even seeing the view of New York Harbor from the Brooklyn Heights Esplanade can be a treat for some seventh-graders; you just have to know if yours is one of them. Browse the chapters, or see the "children" listing in the index for more information.

The New York you or your children first encountered in books can also be fascinating for any age level. Reading is a form of exploration, after all, and it's hard not to be intrigued by the connection of favorite books to the real streets and people of any city, and New York is the scene of countless books. Which scenes you want to revisit will depend on what you've read lately, what you remember most fondly from your own childhood reading, or what you've read recently to your own child. There are a few obvious landmarks, though, such as the Little Red Lighthouse tucked under the George Washington Bridge, and the Plaza Hotel, home of Eloise.

The Little Red Lighthouse and the Great Gray Bridge, by Hildegarde H. Swift, was published in 1942, so it is part of the childhood of several generations of New York–area residents. It's located in Fort Washington Park (178th Street and the Hudson River). It was built in 1921 to serve as a navigational aid, and it was a working lighthouse before and even after the George Washington Bridge was built. In 1947 it was deactivated but preserved as a historic reminder of another era of river life. The lighthouse is now administered by the city's Department of Parks and Recreation; it's open to the public, and New York City Urban Park Rangers conduct tours. It's near the 181st Street stop on the A train.

Eloise, written by Kay Thompson and illustrated by Hilary Knight, also dates to the 1940s, but even more than the Little Red Lighthouse, Eloise continues to be a vivid and contemporary figure. She's a lot of fun to read about (there are several Eloise books in addition to the original), and a walk through the lobby at the Plaza Hotel, at the corner of Fifth Avenue and Central Park South, can add a nice touch to a trip to Central Park or elsewhere in Manhattan. A stop at the **Palm Court** (Plaza Hotel, 768 Fifth Avenue, at Central Park South, 212-546-5350) for afternoon tea or Sunday brunch will bring Eloise even closer and is a delightful experience in its own right.

Any neighborhood that figures in your own family favorites can become a great destination for a custom-planned day trip. When I was growing up, I especially liked the *All-of-a-Kind Family* series by Sydney Taylor. The books are set on the Lower East Side and then in the Bronx; now that the Lower East Side has become so vibrant, it might be fun for other fans of the books to visit the streets so vividly portrayed in these stories of an immigrant family. They've changed, but you can still catch echoes of the past.

Index